Language Handbook

Grade 5

Printed in the United States of America

ISBN 0-15-306866-3

14   073   03 02 01 00

Harcourt

Orlando   Boston   Dallas   Chicago   San Diego

Visit *The Learning Site!*
www.harcourtschool.com

Contents

WRITING

WRITING FORMS

Contents

Contents

HANDWRITING

ADDITIONAL PRACTICE

Using the Handbook

The English language is a practical tool. It can help you face many everyday challenges. You can hammer out a convincing argument or nail down an interesting fact. You can even chisel away at a wordy mess to find a beautiful sentence within.

WHAT IS A HANDBOOK?

If English is a tool, this handbook is the instruction manual. Think of it as a user's guide for words. It gives you advice on getting the most out of this powerful tool. Hints and models will show you what English can do. The advice inside can help you face many daily challenges with confidence and style.

This handbook includes

- ☑ **ideas to help you explore writing assignments.**
- ☑ **examples of writing forms.**
- ☑ **handwriting models and hints.**
- ☑ **grammar rules that won't drive you crazy.**
- ☑ **practice with language.**

"Sometimes the words tell you what you didn't know you knew."
–Lillian Morrison

SECTIONS OF THE HANDBOOK

This handbook has five sections. The first four sections are about writing; writing forms; grammar, usage, and mechanics; and handwriting. In the last section, you get a chance to practice your language skills.

WRITING

You will learn about the writing process. This section can help you explore and complete *any* writing assignment. This section examines planning, drafting, polishing, and publishing your work.

WRITING FORMS

Here you will find models of many common writing forms. Skim through this section to see the kinds of writing included. You'll see everything from stories and poems to letters and tests. The models are grouped according to writing purposes.

GRAMMAR, USAGE, AND MECHANICS

Look in this section to find guidelines about parts of speech, types of sentences, capitalization, and punctuation. Each topic is explained in simple rules. Exercises are included so you can practice what you have learned.

HANDWRITING

Is your writing difficult to read? This section is for you. It shows you how anyone can improve his or her writing.

ADDITIONAL PRACTICE

This section contains exercises in grammar, usage, and mechanics. It can help you test and expand your skills.

"Just as a piano player uses each single note of a piano well, a writer uses each word well."
–Barbara Wersba

HOW TO FIND INFORMATION IN THE HANDBOOK

You can browse through this handbook for hints and advice. You don't need to read from beginning to end. Skim and scan to find topics that look interesting.

Sometimes you will want to look up specific topics. How will you know where to look? Three parts of this book will help you find what you need: the table of contents, the index, and the cross-references.

You will find the **table of contents** right after the title page. It shows the pages on which each section begins. You will also find a mini-table of contents at the beginning of each section.

The **index** is at the back of the book. You can use it to find all references to a specific topic. Topics are listed in alphabetical order.

Some pages have **cross-references.** They will lead you to related topics and additional helpful information.

I need help writing a paragraph about cobras and boa constrictors.

Writing

The Writing Process

Writing is a lot like drawing a picture. Whether you draw or write, you face the same challenge. You need to find the right form for the idea you want to express. Artists are seldom satisfied with the first sketch. More often than not, they begin to make changes almost immediately. They may add a detail here or change a color there. They may even throw away the whole first sketch. There is no one correct way to work. The only "rule" is that the finished product should be the best you can make it.

PREWRITING

Identify your TAP— task, audience, and purpose. Then choose a topic. Gather and organize information about the topic.

DRAFTING

Put your ideas in writing. Don't worry about making mistakes. You can fix them later.

RESPONDING AND REVISING

Reread your writing to see if it meets your purpose. Meet with a partner or with a group to discuss it.

> *"The desire to write grows with writing."*
> *Erasmus*

PROOFREADING

Correct spelling, grammar, usage, mechanics, and capitalization errors.

PUBLISHING

Decide how you want to publish your work. Share your writing.

Planning Tips

Before you actually write, you need to plan your writing. Here are some tips that you can use to organize your thinking and your writing.

UNDERSTANDING TASK, AUDIENCE, AND PURPOSE (TAP)

Before you begin writing, it is a good idea to decide your task, audience, and purpose (TAP). Ask yourself these questions:

Task

- **What am I writing?**

  Do I want to write a letter, a poem, or something else?

Audience

- **For whom am I writing?**

  Am I writing for my teacher, a younger child, a friend, myself, or someone else?

Purpose

- **Why am I writing?**

  Am I writing to persuade someone, to give information, or for another reason?

Your teacher may give you the TAP for an assignment. Sometimes you will decide on your own.

GATHERING YOUR IDEAS

You have your task, audience, and purpose. Now you need to gather ideas. Here are some ways that writers gather ideas.

Brainstorming

- **List your own ideas.**

- **Write freely. Let the ideas flow.**

- **Brainstorm with other people.**

- **Look for writing ideas in**
  magazines   *your journal*
  newspapers   *your portfolio*

Graphic Organizers

Graphic organizers can help you gather ideas or narrow a topic.

Mapping is a good way to find ideas to support a topic.

Reread your journal. You may be surprised at the ideas you stored away there.

rules of the game

my team

Little League Baseball

who can play

my first home run

Making a **story map** can help you organize your ideas for a story.

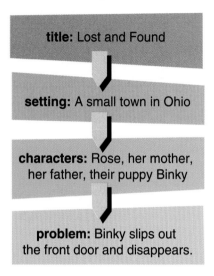

title: Lost and Found

setting: A small town in Ohio

characters: Rose, her mother, her father, their puppy Binky

problem: Binky slips out the front door and disappears.

NARROWING YOUR TOPICS

Use an **inverted pyramid** to work down from broader to narrower topics.

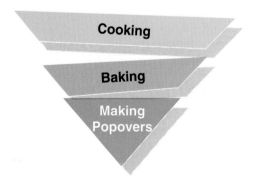

Cooking

Baking

Making Popovers

This topic is too broad.

This is narrower, but still much too broad.

This topic is workable.

Graphic organizers can help you gather ideas and narrow topics. Graphic organizers can also help you organize your ideas.

A **time line** is a kind of outline. It is used to put events and facts in time order.

The First Day of School

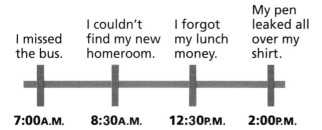

I missed the bus.	I couldn't find my new homeroom.	I forgot my lunch money.	My pen leaked all over my shirt.
7:00 A.M.	8:30 A.M.	12:30 P.M.	2:00 P.M.

A time line can show minutes, hours, days, years, centuries, and so on.

Graphic organizers help you find a workable topic and organize your facts.

A **Venn diagram** shows how two things, such as pets, are alike and how they are different.

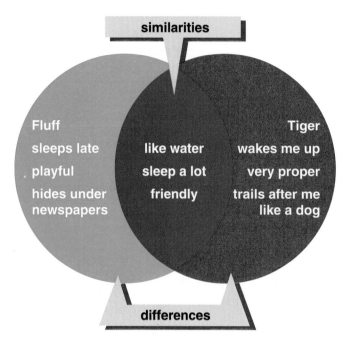

similarities

Fluff
sleeps late
playful
hides under
newspapers

like water
sleep a lot
friendly

Tiger
wakes me up
very proper
trails after me
like a dog

differences

A **cause-effect chart** helps you to see why events happen.

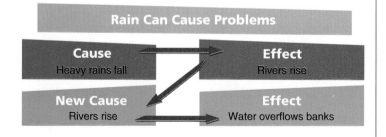

Rain Can Cause Problems

Cause	Effect
Heavy rains fall	Rivers rise

New Cause	Effect
Rivers rise	Water overflows banks

An **outline** can help you organize facts for a report.

Preparing for a Tornado

I. Preparations at home
  A. Choose a safe area to hide in
    1. Locate the southwest corner
       of a basement
    2. Avoid windows
  B. Gather food, transistor radio,
     and flashlight
II. Preparations at school
  A. Follow instructions given by teacher
    1. Move quickly
    2. Do not speak unnecessarily
  B. If outside, lie in a ditch or other
     low place

Roman numerals show main ideas or major sections.

Capital letters show subpoints under main points.

Numbers show details under subpoints.

A **how-to chart** can help you organize steps in time order.

Popover

Materials

large bowl
mixer
12-section muffin tin
4 eggs
1 1/4 cups flour
1 1/4 cups milk
3/4 cup melted butter
1/2 teaspoon salt

Steps

1. Preheat oven to 400° F
2. Beat eggs
3. Stir in milk, butter, and salt
4. Add mixture to flour and
   beat well
5. Pour batter into sections
   of muffin tin
6. Bake at 400° F for 50 minutes

Recipe makes 12 popovers

PREWRITING STRATEGIES

Writing Tips

How do you know when you're ready to write? Try this quick test:

- **Do you like your topic?**

- **Is your plan complete?**

- **Are your fingers itching to write?**

If you answered YES, you're ready. If not, don't worry. It's never too late to change your mind. Try a new topic or a new plan.

GETTING STARTED

Your first goal is to get your ideas down. Don't worry about spelling and grammar. Let the words pour out, as if you were talking with a friend.

- **Choose your favorite writing tool. Will it be a pen, a pencil, a marker, or a computer?**

- **Your prewriting ideas will help you. Do you know where they are? Keep them handy.**

- **Writing doesn't have to be quiet. Talk out your ideas. Read your sentences out loud.**

- **Think about your TAP as you write.**

"Write what you like; there is no other rule."
O. Henry

WRITING AN INTRODUCTION

HEY, LOOK AT *THIS*! An **introduction** draws attention to your writing. It tells your reader what to expect. A great introduction might

- **ask an interesting question.**

- **state a surprising fact or opinion.**

- **explain why your topic is really important.**

WRITING A CONCLUSION

A writer always gets the last word. A **conclusion** presents the last ideas you want the reader to think about. You can wrap up any loose ends and review your main points. Your goal is to leave your reader feeling satisfied. Here are some tips for great conclusions:

- **Summarize your main points.**

- **End with a clever quotation.**

- **Ask a question that will give your reader something to think about.**

Authors often start writing in the middle and then go back and write the introduction.

Polishing Your Writing

Revising, or editing, can make your writing stronger, bolder, sharper, and brighter. You can choose any method of polishing that makes sense to you.

Revising includes:

- **Adding—inserting new words, sentences, and paragraphs.**

- **Replacing—crossing out information and putting new information in its place.**

- **Cutting—getting rid of repeat information or information that is off the topic.**

- **Moving—putting words, sentences, and paragraphs in a more logical order by moving them around.**

Editor's Marks

∧ **Add something.**

✗ **Cut something.**

⌐ **Replace something.**

↻ **Move something.**

HINTS FOR HELPING OTHERS

Listen.

Make specific comments.

Ask about anything that is unclear.

Talk about the parts you like.

REVISING WITH A PARTNER

If you had a choice, would you rather clean up the cafeteria alone or with a friend? You probably agree that having a friend's help would be better. Revising can be a two-person job, too. A revising conference can help you find new and interesting ways to change your writing.

You have strong feelings about your own writing. It might be hard for you to get a clear picture of what you have written. A partner can be a big help. Your partner will bring a "fresh eye"—a new point of view. Reviewing your partner's work can help you think about your own writing, too.

EXPANDING YOUR WRITING

You can expand your writing by **adding details and examples.**

- **Add adjectives and adverbs to make your writing more exciting.**

  I tried to climb the tree.

  I tried **desperately** to climb the **enormous** tree.

- **Add examples to make your writing more specific.**

  It was another one of my kid brother's stunts, **like the time he tried to paint our neighbor's car.**

Adjectives describe nouns. They answer these questions: *What kind? Which one? How many?*

Adverbs usually describe verbs. They tell *how, when, where, how often,* or *to what extent.*

Examples illustrate an idea.

USING FIGURATIVE LANGUAGE

They say a picture is worth a thousand words. So why not try painting pictures with words? Figurative language can help you create lively images.

Similes

- **Similes** compare two unlike things, using the word *like* or *as*. The comparison you make creates an image.

  The waves roared.

  The waves roared **like an angry dragon.**

  I was frightened.

  I was **as frightened as a cat at a dog show.**

Metaphors

- **Metaphors** are like similes except they don't use the words *like* or *as*. They ask the reader to picture one thing as if it were the other thing.

  The ocean was wild.

  The ocean was **a raging beast.**

  After the storm, the beach was clear.

  After the storm, the beach was **a blank page.**

A spicy simile can make a drab sentence stand out like a llama in a laundromat.

USING VIVID WORDS

Use the same old words, and you get the same old writing. Try to use a new word or two every time you write. Use a thesaurus to look for **vivid words.**

For **run**, try *scurry, dash, stream,* or *dart.*

For **old**, try *ancient, antique, prehistoric,* or *dilapidated.*

EDITING WORDY SENTENCES

Could your sentences use a little trimming? Are they a bit sloppy around the edges? Try a little pruning of wordy sentences.

Get rid of unnecessary words.
I was planning to apply to enter the race.
I was planning to enter the race.

Cut words that say the same thing.
I was just starting to begin to run.
I began to run.

Combine words into one idea.
The runner gasped when she saw this really big and really tall hill.
The runner gasped when she saw the enormous hill.

"The most valuable of all talents is that of never using two words when one will do."
Thomas Jefferson

TIPS FOR PROOFREADING

ERROR ALERT! Everybody makes mistakes, and good writers can spot most of their own. Once you have chosen your words, take another look.

Proofreading means looking for mistakes. Here are some tips to help you proofread:

- **Read your work aloud.**

- **Circle all words that could possibly be misspelled. Use a dictionary to find out for sure.**

- **Reread everything you wrote—no skipping. You never know where you'll find a mistake.**

- **Try proofreading in three stages. First, look at spelling. Then, check your grammar. Finally, review punctuation.**

- **Ask a partner to help you spot mistakes.**

- **See pages 91–156 for information about grammar, usage, and mechanics that may help you.**

Proofreader's Marks

☰	Capitalize.
⊙	Add a period.
∧	Add something.
⌃	Add a comma.
ᗉᗉ	Add quotation marks.
℘	Cut something.
⌒	Replace something.
∿	Transpose.
◯	Spell correctly.
℘	Indent paragraph.
/	Make a lowercase letter.

USING COMPUTERS

A computer is a writing tool, just like a pen or a pencil. It can make some parts of writing easier. Here are some tips for computer composers:

Planning

- Write your notes in a separate computer file. Print them out to look at while you write.

Drafting

- Check the screen to see if you typed the right words.

- Type XXX if you can't think of the right word. You can fill it in later.

Revising

- Use *Cut* and *Paste* to rearrange words, sentences, and paragraphs.

Proofreading

- Use the spelling checker, but be careful! It can't catch everything. (Homophones are especially tricky.) It would find nothing wrong with this sentence: Hiss speech maid me paws too think.

Publishing

- You can change the size of letters. Give your work a big headline. Give your name a by-line.

Always keep a hard copy of your work. (That means a copy on paper.) SAVE your work often.

PROOFREADING STRATEGIES

A REVISED AND PROOFREAD DRAFT

My father dared me to stop watching TV for a week. Monday was ~~bad~~ *miserable*. Tuesday was worse. I felt ~~awful~~ *torture* like a jockey without a horse. On thursday I snapped. I just had to watch my favorite show. I grabbed the (remoat) but Dad said, "I told you so." That did it. No TV for me.

I read books and drew pictures. I found ~~my~~ ways to fill my extra time. The week was actually fun. Will I give up television forever? Not a chance! But I'll probably watch a little less.

Replace: *Miserable* and *torture* are more descriptive than *bad* and *worse.*

Add: A simile creates an interesting image.

Capitalize: Days of the week always start with a capital letter.

Spell: A dictionary shows that *remoat* is not right.

Quotation Marks: They go around Dad's exact words.

Cut: The word *my* is unnecessary.

Move: This order makes more sense.

Add: An exclamation adds excitement!

FINAL DRAFT MODEL

One Week Without

My father dared me, so I had to try. I thought it would be easy. All I had to do was stop watching TV for a week. Monday was miserable. Tuesday was torture. I felt like a jockey without a horse. On Thursday, I snapped. I just had to watch my favorite show. I grabbed the remote, but Dad said, "I told you so." That did it. No TV for me.

I found ways to fill my extra time. I read books, drew pictures, and even wrote an overdue thank-you letter to Grandma. The week was actually fun. Will I give up television forever? Not a chance! But I'll probably watch a little less and do a little more.

A catchy title prepares the reader.

A new introduction sets up the story.

A neat copy is much easier to read.

The last paragraph has a new example and ends with a satisfying prediction.

Publishing Your Writing

Most writing is meant to be read. Publishing means sharing your work with others. You might make a neat copy and share it with a friend. You can publish without paper, too. Act out a story or give a speech, and you are publishing your work.

PUBLISHING ON YOUR OWN

- Make a tape recording of your writing project, with sound effects.

- Send your writing off on a computer disk or by modem to someone you know who has a computer.

- Read your work out loud for an invited audience.

- Add some drawings to turn your project into a comic book or a brochure.

- Write your project as a letter and send it to someone you know.

- Submit your writing to a magazine or newspaper. Keep a copy for your own files before you send it away.

Words at Work

newspapers

movies

plays

bulletin boards

posters

songs

catalogs

postcards

comic strips

PUBLISHING WITH A GROUP

- Make a class video. Let everyone read a sample of his or her writing. Videotape pictures that bring the writing to life.

- Start your own writers' group. Put out a newsletter or magazine with catchy headlines and interesting pictures.

- Put together a book or a pamphlet. Your school library might put it on display for others to read.

- Hold a panel discussion. Invite members of another class to listen to you present and discuss your writing.

- Organize a writing contest. Choose a panel of judges and decide on the rules. Create a special booklet to showcase the winning works.

Some Publishing Tools

paper

poster

audiotape

videotape

stamps and envelopes

computer disks

fax machine

voice

Writing Approaches

You write almost every day. You might write

school notes	a phone message
a shopping list	a birthday card
test answers	a class schedule

There are many ways to write. The choice is up to you. Try a variety of them. Experiment! You may find a way to write that you really like.

WRITING IN A GROUP

Writing in a group, or collaborative writing, can produce surprising results. A group has the combined writing power of all its members. Here are a few hints for ways to write with others:

- Listen to each other. Share your ideas.

- Assign tasks or roles for each group member. Make sure everyone has something to do.

- Keep your goal in mind as you work. Stay on course to keep your group productive.

- Use a tape recorder to keep track of group brainstorming.

- If you're working on a story or a play, try giving each group member a different character. A little acting might help a lot.

Group Writing Roles

Recorder — gets the words down

Reader — reads the words aloud

Checker — makes sure the facts are correct

Questioner — raises questions; expresses different viewpoints

SHARED WRITING

Shared writing is writing with a teacher or a family member. You talk out loud, and your partner writes down your ideas. A good partner asks questions that keep you on track. Here are some questions a partner might ask:

Questions About Topics

- **What is your task?**
- **Is your topic broad enough?**
- **Is it too broad?**
- **What do you already know about it?**

Questions About Words

- **What does this mean?**
- **Is this the best word?**
- **Are you happy with it?**

WRITING TO LEARN

Words help you think. **Writing to learn** can help you guide your thoughts. You can write lists, notes, and messages to yourself to get your thoughts flowing. Even if you throw out your writing, the thoughts will remain in your brain.

Brain Training

Comparing Take notes about different brands of sneakers to find the best pair at the best price.

Classifying Keep a list of your music or video collection. How will you organize your list?

Note Page

You are writing to learn when you take notes. The trick is to keep thinking while you write. One way is to write your notes in two columns. The left-hand side is for facts you are studying. The right-hand side is for questions or ideas of your own.

Animals	
Invertebrates (have no backbone)	What is the difference between a plant and an animal?
jellyfish	
worms	Squid and octopus go here?
lobsters	
sponges	Sponges are alive?
Vertebrates (have a backbone) cold-blooded snakes, fish, lizards	Is their blood really cold? These are all scaly.
warm-blooded birds, mammals	like my gerbil

Writing Forms

Writing to Entertain or Express

What is your purpose for writing? You could write **to entertain** your readers—to amuse them, thrill them, or make them cry. You can also write **to express** yourself—to bring your feelings, thoughts, or ideas to the surface. When you write to entertain or express, ask yourself these questions:

PREWRITING

Choosing a Topic

- **What is my favorite kind of writing? Is it a story, a poem, or a play? Why?**

- **Has anything happened to me that a reader might find amusing or exciting?**

- **What makes me special?**

Gathering Information

- **Who will the main characters be?**

- **Do I know enough about the setting?**

- **Would a story map help me work out the plot?**

- **Would brainstorming help me find words to describe my topic?**

"I care not who knows it—I write for the general amusement."
Sir Walter Scott

DRAFTING

- Will I start writing at the beginning, in the middle, or with the ending?

- How does my writing sound when I read it aloud?

- Will I use dialogue?

RESPONDING AND REVISING

- Are my descriptions vivid and interesting?

- Will the writing be clear to my audience?

- Can I add more or better details?

PROOFREADING

- Did I indent every paragraph?

- Have I used quotation marks when needed?

PUBLISHING

- What is the best way to reach my audience?

- Is my final version neat enough to be read easily?

ENTERTAINING AND EXPRESSIVE WRITING MODELS

MODEL: STORY

*A **story** has a setting, characters, and a plot. The characters and events in a **realistic story** are believable.*

City Birds

The introduction tells you about the characters and the setting.

Sandra pointed her camera at the very top of the tall silver skyscraper. She waited patiently. Her sister Ana was not so patient.

"I'm bored and I'm hot," said Ana.

Dialogue tells the reader what the characters are like through what they are saying.

"Shh. The falcon will come out today," said Sandra. "I know it will."

"Will not! I'm hungry. Let's go," wailed Ana.

Sandra ignored her. A peregrine falcon was supposed to be living at the top of this office building. Sandra was determined to get a picture of it.

This sentence tells the main character's goal. That's one way of thinking about a story's *problem*.

Suddenly, Ana cried out, "Look! There it is!" Sandra turned around quickly. Ana was pointing across the street at a big pigeon.

"That's not a falcon," said Sandra. "Falcons are beautiful."

"I think that bird is beautiful."

"It is not," Sandra shouted. "It's ugly! You can't tell the difference between a falcon and a pigeon."

Ana turned away and started to sniffle. Sandra was sorry she had gotten so angry. She went back to looking through her camera lens. The sisters sat back-to-back. They were as silent as two bookends.

Then Ana saw something. "Sandra," she whispered nervously.

"What is it?" snapped Sandra.

"Look up there, at that other building."

Ana pointed at the building across the street. Way up at the top, a small shadow swooped to a ledge. Sandra looked through her zoom lens. It was the falcon. She had been watching the wrong building.

"That's it!" she said. "Take a look." She handed her sister the camera. Ana looked through the lens.

"That's a beautiful bird, too," she said.

Sandra laughed. She let Ana push the button. It was going to be a beautiful picture.

See "Dialogue," page 153.

MODEL: FOLKTALE

Folktales are meant to be shared aloud. Many of them have elements of magic. Sometimes they teach a lesson, too.

The Clumsy Juggler

Hugo was a juggler. He was really good except for one little problem. He dropped everything. One day, he set up a sign. It said, "Hugo, the World's Best Juggler!" A crowd quickly gathered.

He dropped balls. "Boo," said the crowd. Then he dropped some sticks. "Boo, boo," said the crowd. Hugo was sad. He picked up his things and dumped them into a fountain. The moon felt sorry for Hugo. When Hugo fell asleep, the moon took out his paints.

The next day, Hugo tried again. Another crowd gathered. Hugo dropped everything again. The crowd laughed and gave him silver.

Hugo was confused. Then he looked at his sign. Now it said, "Hugo, the World's Clumsiest Juggler." Hugo looked up at the moon and smiled.

repetition to create humor

magical character and events

problem solved

Tall tales use exaggeration and humor to tell unbelievable stories. They stretch the truth so far it breaks.

friendly, chatty language

unbelievable events

exaggerated claims

Glenda Garoo

The longest hair I ever knew was on Glenda Garoo. She could wrap it around her head eighty-two times. Long ago, she had regular hair like me and you. But then it grew.

You see, one day, Glenda's little boy, Hugh, fell down a well. Glenda stared down the well. She tried to think of a plan. She thought so hard that her brain fizzed with energy. That energy was so strong that it made her hair grow. The next thing you know, little Hugh was climbing up her hair. Glenda was so glad, she promised she'd never cut it. And she never did.

See "Comparing with Adjectives," pages 126–127.

MODEL: RHYMED POEM

ABAB rhyme pattern

quick, playful rhythm

*In a **rhymed poem,** sounds are repeated at the ends of some lines. The rhyming lines usually follow a pattern.*

My Pet Poem

I wanted a cat
    but I had to be smart
When I asked for
        permission from Mama.
I knew that she'd never
        agree from the start
So I begged her instead
        for a llama.

Then I begged for a moose
        and I begged for a bat
And I begged for
        a fat crocodile.
When Mama suggested
        I might like a cat
I said, "Maybe"
        and swallowed my smile.

See "Using Figurative Language," page 24.

MODEL: UNRHYMED POEM

An **unrhymed poem** *creates a feeling using rhythm, figurative language, and imagery. The way the words look on the page is important, too.*

Reading in Bed

image painted with
carefully selected words

Under my covers
my flashlight turns my book to silver
until my father says
"put out
that light."

interesting arrangement
of words

Repetition creates
rhythm.

Under my covers
my dreams are silver flashes of my book
until my mother says
"time to wake up."

See "Using Vivid Words," page 25.

MODEL: PLAY

Plays are written to be acted out. Dialogue, or the words the characters say, tells the story. Stage directions are written in parentheses. They tell a reader about the characters' actions and emotions.

Only Kidding

cast list

Characters
MARIE, a practical joker
JODI, Marie's friend
GLENN, a new student

setting

<u>**(Jodi and Marie are eating lunch in the school cafeteria.)**</u>

JODI: Hey, look. There's Glenn.

MARIE: Let's play a joke on him, OK?

JODI: Sure. Hey, Glenn, come here.

<u>**(Glenn sits down.)**</u>

Character names show
who is talking.

GLENN: Hi, Marie. Hi, Jodi.

MARIE: Mom always makes me peanut butter, and I hate peanut butter.

GLENN: I have tomato and cheese.

MARIE: That sounds good. You want to trade?

GLENN: (<u>hesitantly</u>) I guess so.

Stage directions show action.	<u>(Glenn bites into his sandwich and looks amazed. Marie and Jodi laugh.)</u>
	GLENN: Yuck! This isn't peanut butter. It's tuna fish!
	JODI: You should see your face!
	GLENN: <u>(gasping)</u> I'm...allergic...to...tuna...fish!
	<u>(He faints.)</u>
Adverbs show how a line should be said.	**MARIE:** <u>(nervously)</u> Oh, no! Now look what you've done!
	JODI: Me? It was you who did it!
	MARIE: What are we gonna do?
	<u>(Glenn sits up.)</u>
Ending wraps up the story.	**GLENN:** <u>(cheerfully)</u> Only kidding. I love tuna fish. But that'll teach you to play silly tricks!

See "Writing in a Group," page 32, and "Adverbs," pages 140–143.

Writing to Describe

When you write **to describe,** you paint your audience an exact picture. It's important to be as specific as you can. The right adjectives, nouns, and verbs can help your audience picture exactly what you are talking about. These questions may help you when you write a description:

PREWRITING

Choosing a Topic

- **Have I seen anything that was really amazing?**

- **Have I met anyone who was fascinating?**

- **Is my idea too broad? Can I narrow my focus to one part of it?**

Gathering Information

- **What words come to mind when I think of this subject?**

- **Will looking at pictures in a book or magazine help me get ideas?**

- **Could drawing a picture of my subject help me think about how it looks?**

- **If my subject is a person, can I describe how he or she walks, talks, and smiles?**

"I think of myself... as one who reflects reality, paints a picture."
Judy Blume

DRAFTING

- Can I introduce my subject in an interesting way?

- What time order will I use to describe my subject?

- Can I save a special, important detail for the conclusion?

RESPONDING AND REVISING

- Can I replace any nouns or verbs with more specific ones?

- Would different adjectives or adverbs help me describe my subject better?

- Will someone who has never seen or met my subject get a clear picture of what he, she, or it is like?

PROOFREADING

- Are any words misspelled?

- Did I use commas in a series correctly?

PUBLISHING

- How can I best reach my audience?

- Would an illustration help my description?

- Would I like to send my description to a friend or relative?

PURPOSES FOR WRITING

MODEL: DESCRIPTIVE PARAGRAPH

title

topic sentence

Sensory details can appeal to all the senses: sight, hearing, smell, touch, and taste.

A **descriptive paragraph** tells about one specific topic. The topic should be narrow enough to describe in a handful of sentences.

Grandfather's Bread

My grandfather's bread is both delicious to eat and gorgeous to look at. He brings a new loaf every Saturday. You can smell the warm bread even before he walks in. The dough is always twisted like a lock of braided hair. He paints the top with egg to make it dark mahogany brown. Then he sprinkles it with tasty sesame seeds. It looks almost too good to eat, but we always do. The crust is crisp and crunchy. The inside is soft, warm, and airy.

See "Using Vivid Words," page 25, and "Adjective and Proper Adjective," pages 124–125.

*You can describe a more complicated subject in a **descriptive essay**. Each paragraph in a descriptive essay focuses on one part of the whole picture. One way to arrange your ideas is to use spatial order—that is, you might describe your subject from top to bottom, from left to right, or from the middle out.*

A Spanish American Street Fair

introduction

Last week, our block was closed off for a street fair. Spanish and American flags hung on all the telephone poles, and red and yellow streamers decorated every booth.

explanation of unusual terms

The first booths on the block sold Spanish American food. One booth sold spicy paella from a giant pan. It is made of rice, mussels, shrimp, and squid. At the next booth, you could smell empanadas, which are made of dough that is filled with beef or fish. Other booths sold gazpacho, a cold tomato soup.

The next booths tempted people to play games to win giant stuffed animals. One game booth was for throwing balls at milk bottles. Another game booth was for squirting water pistols into balloons.

Spatial order organizes the description.

In the middle of the block there was a band platform set up. Musicians played Spanish music on accordions and guitars all day long. Then some dancers performed a flamenco dance. This is a dance with lots of quick, clicking steps.

The other half of the block was set up for selling things. Some things were everyday items, like pillows, T-shirts, and books. There were also some unusual items made in Spain. You could buy painted plates, carved leather bags, and beautiful beaded jewelry.

adjectives used to compare

The conclusion gives an overall impression.

At the very end of the block sat a little Ferris wheel. It wasn't very high, but from the top you could see the whole scene perfectly. Our block was a blur of people, banners, music, and booths. What a party!

See "Expanding Your Writing," page 23, and "Comparing with Adjectives," pages 126–127.

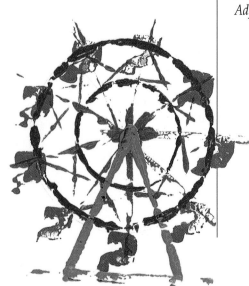

sensory details

figurative language

vivid verbs

When you want to describe a person, you can write a **character sketch.** You can tell your reader a lot about someone in just a few words, including how your subject looks, sounds, and acts.

Ms. Tuva is the checker at our corner grocery store. When you first see her, she looks sad. Her eyes are dark and always half-closed. Her face is very still. But when she starts talking, you can tell she's really friendly. Her voice is high, like a parakeet's. Every sentence is a song. She chatters about school, her family, and the weather. Her face never changes, but she sounds very excited. When you wave good-bye, she lifts her hand halfway and jiggles it a little. That's about as dramatic as Ms. Tuva gets.

See "Using Figurative Language," page 24, and "Action Verb," page 129.

Writing to Inform

You write **to inform** when you want to tell your audience about something you know. You might inform your readers about interesting facts or about how to do something. These questions may help you when your purpose is to inform:

PREWRITING

Choosing a Topic

- What topics do I know about?

- What topics do I want to find out about?

- Is my topic too broad or too narrow? Will there be too much or too little to say about it?

Gathering Information

- Where can I look to find more information?

- Who can I ask that might be able to help me?

- Would a chart help me organize my ideas? How will I set it up?

PURPOSES FOR WRITING

DRAFTING

- What main idea do I want to share with my audience?

- How can I best use my notes? Would it help to mark them off as I use them?

RESPONDING AND REVISING

- Does my introduction introduce the topic?

- Are my facts accurate?

- Does the order of my writing make sense?

PROOFREADING

- Have I capitalized all proper nouns?

- Which words should I look up in a dictionary?

PUBLISHING

- How would I like to share my work with others?

- Would visual aids help an oral delivery?

- What magazine or newspaper might be interested in publishing my work?

MODEL: PERSONAL NARRATIVE

You can write about something that really happened to you in a **personal narrative.** Choose a memorable event and tell how you felt about it. Tell the beginning, middle, and ending of your story.

First-person pronouns (*I* and *my*) refer to the author.

My pen pal, Tami, changed my life forever. I wrote her a letter when I was sad. I told her about the big race at school. I use a wheelchair, so I can't run. I told Tami how left out I felt.

details in time order

She wrote back right away. She told me about the Special Olympics. It's a great organization for people who are physically challenged.

I called our local chapter. They hold wheelchair races. I was so excited that I entered right away. I wrote Tami a letter about my very first race. I think everybody should have a pen pal like Tami.

Conclusion makes a general statement.

See "Writing a Conclusion," page 21, and "Pronouns," pages 119–123.

MODEL: PARAGRAPH OF INFORMATION

An **information paragraph** tells the reader about one specific topic. You can write about a topic you know well, or you can research an interesting subject. The paragraph may include opinions if they are supported by facts.

topic sentence

supporting details

Conclusion includes an opinion supported by the paragraph.

The Library of Congress is the world's largest national library. It has more than 97 million items, including books, pamphlets, maps, photographs, and recordings. It has works in more than 450 languages. One way that the library gets books is through the United States copyright laws. Every work that is copyrighted must be submitted to the Library of Congress. So if you ever apply for a copyright, your manuscript will be on file in one of the most amazing libraries in the world.

See "Writing to Learn Note Page," page 34.

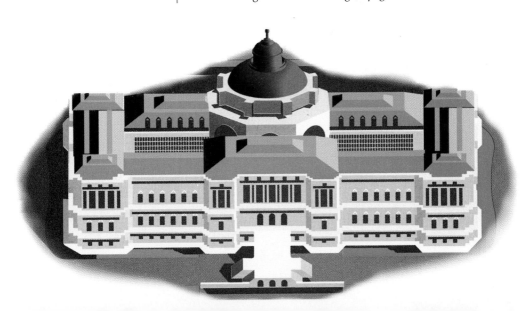

MODEL: HOW-TO PARAGRAPH

*A **how-to paragraph** is a perfect way to give a quick set of directions or some helpful advice. Clear writing will help a reader follow your advice, so avoid wordy and confusing sentences.*

How to Improve Your Soccer Kick

good advice

clear, direct instructions

Imperative sentences give directions.

Here are a few tricks that will help you shoot goals in soccer. Remember that the object of the game is to score. If you get a chance, take it. Look at the center of the ball when you kick it. Watch your foot hit the ball. Then follow through with your leg <u>and</u> your eyes. Put as much of your weight into the shot as you can without losing your balance. The best shooters are almost entirely off the ground when they kick. With a little practice, you'll be kicking better than ever.

See "Imperative Sentences," page 96, and "Editing Wordy Sentences," page 25.

You can tell a reader how to follow a series of directions in a **how-to essay.** *The reader has to be able to follow along easily, so the order of your steps is important.*

A Personal Paper Doll

You can be a real doll! It's easy. Just follow these steps.

First, ask a friend to take your picture. Stand in front of something blank, like a white wall. Make sure your feet are in the shot.

After you get the film developed, choose your favorite picture and have it enlarged to about 8 inches high.

Next, glue your picture onto heavy cardboard. When the glue is dry, cut out your picture. Use a lump of clay to make a base, and set your picture in it.

You can now use cloth, paper, and glitter to dress up your doll. Make clothes, eyeglasses, hats, or shoes.

A personal paper doll makes an enjoyable toy or a good gift. It's an easy and amusing project for any time of year.

See "Prepositions," pages 145–147.

Steps include good advice.

time-order words

Prepositional phrases make information more specific.

MODEL: PARAGRAPH THAT COMPARES

words of comparison:
too, both, either, and *neither*

logical order of ideas

You can write a **comparison paragraph** to show how two things are alike. Choose two things that have a lot in common but are not exactly the same. A comparison can show how two things are related.

If you like to play chess, you might like go, too. The two games have a lot in common. Go is a Chinese strategy game. Both chess and go have been played for hundreds and hundreds of years. They started out as war games. The object of each game is to capture the other player's pieces. Both games are played on boards divided into squares. You need to use strategy to win either game. Neither one is hard to learn, but both can take a lifetime to master.

MODEL: PARAGRAPH THAT CONTRASTS

*You can write a **contrast paragraph** to show how two things are different. Choose subjects that have something in common, even though you are contrasting them. It wouldn't make sense to contrast a fish and a boomerang. It would make more sense to contrast a boomerang and a paper airplane, or two kinds of fish.*

topic sentence

adjectives used to contrast

Although they are both used for drawing, charcoal and pastels are very different. Pastels come in a lot of different colors, but charcoal is usually black. Pastels are made of oil and pigment. Most charcoal is made from wood. It is easier to erase charcoal than to erase pastels. Charcoal can be very hard or very soft, but pastels are always soft. You can buy charcoal in sticks or in pencils. Pastels only come in sticks.

See "Comparing with Adjectives," pages 126–127.

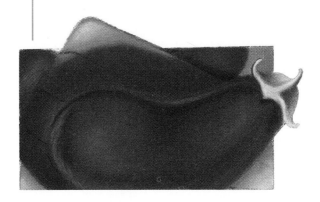

EXPOSITORY WRITING

MODEL: WRITING FOR MATH

Specific steps explain solution process.

Conclusion answers the question.

*When you write for **math,** you often answer a question and tell how you found your answer. Your writing should be as specific as possible. Explain each step of your thinking.*

Question: One ounce of unpopped popcorn makes about 2 cups of popcorn. How much unpopped popcorn would you use to make a popcorn snack for your entire class? Explain how you found your estimate.

I think that each student should get $\frac{1}{2}$ cup of popcorn. There are 32 children in our class. I multiplied 32 by $\frac{1}{2}$ and got 16. That means we need 16 cups of popcorn. Since 1 ounce makes 2 cups, I figured out that 2 ounces would make 4 cups, 3 ounces would make 6 cups, and so on. To make 16 cups, we would need to use 8 ounces of popcorn. Just to make sure everyone has enough, I would use 9 ounces of popcorn.

MODEL: WRITING FOR SCIENCE

Science writing includes lab and research reports. Check your facts to make sure they are accurate. Write clearly and precisely.

Introduction explains the reason for the experiment.

This report is about my goldfish experiment. I tried to test my hypothesis that it is possible to train a goldfish. The experiment began 3 weeks ago.

Body explains the experiment and its results.

For the experiment, I tapped on the bowl before each feeding. At first the fish ignored my tapping. It came to the surface only when I put in the food.

After 8 days, I noticed that the fish was beginning to come to the top as soon as I tapped on the bowl. Now, after 21 days, the fish always comes to the top of the bowl as soon as I tap. Even if I do not feed it right away, it still comes to the top.

Conclusion makes a generalization and a prediction.

This experiment proves that goldfish can be trained. For my next experiment, I will see if the goldfish will learn to respond to light instead of tapping. I think it will work.

See "Writing an Introduction" and "Writing a Conclusion," page 21.

NEWS STORY
INTERVIEW TECHNIQUES

An audience reads a news story to find out current information. The story can answer the questions *who, what, when, where, why*, and *how.* One good way to find information for a news story is to **interview** somebody knowledgeable. Try these hints to become an expert interviewer:

- Begin by writing the subject's name at the top of your page. Then list the facts you already know.

- Write a list of questions *before* your interview.

- Take notes while you talk. You can also tape-record your interview.

- Listen to your subject's responses. These will often make you think of more questions.

Simon Levy, the winner of the Video Showdown

Who?	1. Who did you play against?
What?	2. What games did you play?
When?	3. When did you first start playing?
Where?	4. Where was the contest held?
Why?	5. Why do you think you won?
How?	6. How did you learn to play?

*A **news story** has a headline, a lead paragraph, and a body. The lead paragraph introduces the topic. The body gives the rest of the information about the current event.*

headline

Simon Levy Wins Video Duel

lead to tell *who, what, where, and when*

Simon Levy won yesterday's Video Showdown at Arcadia, the new game arcade. The contest attracted fifty-four players. Simon played forty rounds to win the grand prize: a one-month free pass to Arcadia.

body

Levy attends fifth grade at Bowman Elementary School. He started playing video games when he was four. His older brother coached him.

Levy was modest about his victory. "I got lucky in the last round," he said. "Star Quest was selected for the final. That's my best game."

Alisha Jackson, the runner-up, said that it took more than luck. "This guy is amazing," she said.

The owner of Arcadia says she plans to have another Video Showdown next year.

See "News Story," page 62, and "Dialogue," page 153.

MODEL: RESEARCH REPORT OUTLINE

An **outline** can help you organize information for a research report. An outline uses Roman numerals for topics, capital letters for subtopics, and numbers for details. You should include at least two subtopics for every topic.

Carnivorous Plants

main topic

two or more subtopics for each topic

details

I. Why carnivorous plants eat insects
   A. They need nitrogen
   B. Wetlands have very little nitrogen
   C. Insects contain nitrogen
II. Kinds of carnivorous plants
   A. Plants that move
      1. Venus's-flytrap
      2. Bladderworts
   B. Plants that do not move
      1. Pitcher plants
      2. Butterworts
III. Why some carnivorous plants are becoming rare
   A. Wetlands are decreasing
   B. The plants can't survive in other areas

EXPOSITORY WRITING

MODEL: RESEARCH REPORT

*A **research report** gives information about a topic. Use a variety of sources to find information. Remember to explain unfamiliar terms.*

title

explanation of the term *carnivorous*

topic sentences followed by supporting details

facts presented in a logical order

Carnivorous Plants

Plants that eat insects are called <u>carnivorous</u>. All plants need nitrogen to survive. Most carnivorous plants live in wetland areas. The soil there has very little nitrogen. Carnivorous plants get their nitrogen by eating insects.

Some carnivorous plants move to catch their prey. The Venus's-flytrap can shut its leaves around an insect. The two leaves snap together like a clam. Bladderworts use water pressure to trap underwater insects.

Other plants catch insects without moving. Pitcher plants use pitfall traps. Insects are attracted to the plant, fall into the pool, and drown. Butterworts have sticky parts that act like flypaper.

Many carnivorous plants are becoming rare. Wetland areas in the United States are shrinking. Without these areas, carnivorous plants will not survive.

Writing to Persuade

You will write **to persuade** when you want to make your audience believe that your point of view is right. You need to give your audience some proof. Supporting details can help. You might answer these questions as you work on a piece of persuasive writing:

PREWRITING

Choosing a Topic

- What are my strongest opinions?

- What movies, books, or magazines do I think are really good (or bad)?

- Will I be able to persuade a reader that I am right?

Gathering Information

- How did I form my opinion?

- Where can I look for supporting details?

- Can I find any quotations that support my idea?

- Do I have at least three points I can use to support my opinion?

DRAFTING

- How will I state my point of view?

- Which of my supporting details is strongest? Will I put that one first or last?

RESPONDING AND REVISING

- Is my language strong and direct?

- Will my audience be convinced? Would more reasons or evidence help?

- Did I include any unnecessary details?

PROOFREADING

- Have I double-checked my spelling?

- Did I punctuate direct quotations correctly?

PUBLISHING

- Would an oral or a written presentation be more effective?

- What is the best way to reach my audience?

PERSUASIVE WRITING MODELS

MODEL: PERSUASIVE PARAGRAPH

A **persuasive paragraph** presents a short, clear argument. The writer tries to convince an audience that an opinion is correct. Facts and reasons are used to support the argument.

thesis statement

reasons that support the opinion

I think that the Emerson High School pool should be open at night for our community. There is no public pool in town. The high school swim team doesn't use the pool after six o'clock. The pool could be open every night until nine. Everyone would have a chance to use the pool, including students who are not yet in high school. The school is already open for night classes. The only additional expenses would be a lifeguard and a security person, and I think that their fees could be paid for by community fund-raising. It is a shame to leave this beautiful pool unused.

See "Expanding Your Writing," page 23.

MODEL: PERSUASIVE ESSAY

*You may want to write a **persuasive essay** when you have a major point to make. Begin with a clear thesis statement. Each paragraph can offer a different reason to support your opinion.*

thesis statement

    I think that commercials should be banned from Saturday-morning television. It is unfair to expose children to advertising. The ads on Saturday are the worst.

supporting ideas

    Little children do not have critical abilities. They believe everything they see. Right now, they see a lot of ads. In fact, the average American sees about 3,000 ads every day.

    The commercials on Saturday mornings are designed by adults to make children want things. It is not surprising that they work. Adults know how to make products look irresistible to children. This is not fair.

negatives used to emphasize points

    Teachers can help. They can use class time to teach children how to see through ads. That way, they will be prepared to resist the 125 ads they see every hour on Saturdays.

See "Editing Wordy Sentences," page 25, and "Negatives," page 144.

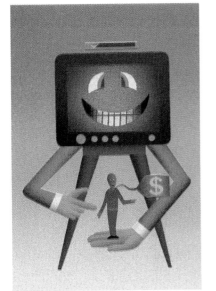

MODEL: BOOK REVIEW

*How can you share your opinion of a book? A **book review** tells how a reader felt about a book. The reader discusses details from the book that support his or her opinion.*

name of book underlined; author identified

Writer supports opinion with details from book.

recommendation

The House of Dies Drear by Virginia Hamilton is an exciting story. I never knew what was going to happen next. I liked it because it was so unpredictable.

It tells the story of Thomas Small and his family. They move into an old house that was once a station on the Underground Railroad. The house is supposed to be haunted by the ghosts of Dies Drear and two slaves who were murdered.

I thought the book was going to be a typical ghost story. Then a mysterious character named Mr. Pluto shows up. He wants to protect the historic house from greedy neighbors. They want to steal its treasures.

Anyone who likes a suspenseful story will like this book. It also has a lot of interesting information about life in America before the Civil War. I can't wait to read the sequel, The Mystery of Drear House.

See "Titles," page 154.

PERSUASIVE/EXPOSITORY

*Reviewers share their opinions with readers. A **movie** or **TV review** follows the same rules as a book review. A good review tells an audience what to expect without giving everything away.*

title of movie underlined

opinions

adjectives used to compare

Even though it was made in 1933, <u>King Kong</u> is an electrifying movie. It doesn't seem old-fashioned at all. I don't usually like black-and-white movies, but I loved this one.

Some scientists discover Kong on a remote island. They capture him and bring him to New York City. Of course, they can't keep him tied up for long.

The acting is very believable — especially that of Kong! The special effects are so convincing that I forgot Kong was just a model. Sometimes the movie looks like a documentary.

The final scene is the most famous. Kong climbs to the top of the Empire State Building. It is a very exciting climax. I have my doubts about the ending, though. I wish the writers had found a way to make it happier. Still, this movie is certainly worth seeing.

See "Comparing with Adjectives," pages 126–127, and "Titles," page 154.

SPEECH OR ORAL REPORT WITH VISUALS

Tongue Twister

Listeners seldom sleep unless speakers sound insincere, so speak simply.

Giving a speech is a great way to persuade an audience to your point of view. Hearing a persuasive speech can be more convincing than just reading it to yourself. Here are some tips for preparing an effective speech:

- **You don't need to memorize your speech. Use note cards or an outline.**

- **Try to think of visuals that can communicate ideas. Pictures, graphs, charts, and slides can really seize your audience's interest.**

- **Practice. Try out your speech on a member of your family, or even your dog. You'll be much more relaxed if you've practiced first.**

Consider these tips when you give your speech:

- **Speak clearly and don't rush. The first step to convincing an audience is having your words understood.**

- **Make eye contact with your audience. They want to see your face, not the top of your head.**

- **Explain your visuals carefully.**

- **Answer questions politely and thoroughly.**

thesis statement at end of paragraph

visuals used to support opinion

dramatic ending

Hello. I am here to talk about our school mascot. We have been the Newsbrook Braves since 1932. The name may have been a good idea back then, but I think it's time for a change.

Many people agree that the name seems to show insensitivity to Native Americans. In fact, I took a poll of one hundred students in our school. This graph shows the results. As you can see, almost 75 percent of the people think we should change.

I propose that we have a school contest. Anyone can submit an idea. A fair vote will decide what our new mascot is to be. I would like to start the contest by unveiling my own proposal for our new mascot. Here it is: the Newsbrook Barracudas!

See "Note-Taking," page 84.

Everyday Writing

You are writing anytime you jot words down or fill out a form. In fact, most people write something every day. It may be just a few notes, a quick card, or a letter. When your purpose is **everyday writing**, you can use the writing process to help you communicate clearly.

Could you go through an entire day without a pen or pencil?

PREWRITING

Choosing a Topic

- **What is my main goal for this piece of writing?**

- **Am I writing for myself or for an audience?**

Gathering Information

- **Do I need to find any information before I write? Where can I find it?**

- **Would a word web help me explore ideas?**

DRAFTING

- **What is my most important point?**

- **How will I organize my ideas?**

RESPONDING AND REVISING

- Did I leave anything out?

- If I'm writing for myself, have I included enough details so that I will remember what I was thinking?

- If I'm writing for an audience, will they understand what I mean?

PROOFREADING

- If I'm writing for myself, are my abbreviations easy to understand?

- If I'm writing for an audience, did I spell everything correctly?

PUBLISHING

- Will I share my writing with someone else?

- Would it make sense to make a neater copy?

MODEL: PERSONAL JOURNAL

You can write your personal thoughts in a **personal journal.** The writing in this kind of journal is not meant to be shared. A journal can be your private place for writing down dreams, feelings, or thoughts.

date of entry

Informal language includes incomplete sentences and personal abbreviations.

Doodles can express ideas too.

Saturday, December 28

I just got back from celebrating Kwanzaa at Gloria's. It was inspiring. Everyone was really happy. There were lots and lots of candles all lit at once. It was beautiful, like looking at stars in the sky.

We sang songs and people told stories. Gloria's great-great-great-grandmother (maybe one more great) was born in Africa. The stories made me think about how lucky I am to be living today instead of 200 years ago. Next year I want Mom and Dad to come with me.

DESCRIPTIVE/NARRATIVE

A **dialogue journal** contains an exchange of writing between a student and teacher. You can write about anything that happens in class. Then your teacher responds to your entry. A dialogue journal can be a good way to clear up confusion.

speaking directly to teacher

problem identified

May 29, 199___

Geometry is really hard for me. I have trouble when you use shape names. I can never remember how many sides hexagons have. I can remember pentagons because of the five-sided building in Washington.

Mandy

teacher's response in writing

May 30, 199___

You're on the right track! Your way of remembering _pentagon_ is perfect. Try to think up your own word associations. I remember that a _hexagon_ has _six_ sides because they both have the letter _x_ in them.

Mrs. Spencer

See "Writing to Learn," page 33.

MODEL: FRIENDLY LETTER

A ***friendly letter*** *is written to someone you know. You can write anything you might say in person. A letter can be entertaining, descriptive, informative, or persuasive.*

heading

2561 S. Park Blvd.
Boulder, CO 80322
May 26, 199-

greeting

Dear Zack,

body

How are you? It seems like ages since we saw each other. I guess it was last Thanksgiving. It looks as if we might visit you this summer. Mom isn't sure if she can get the time off. She's been _really_ busy at work. Remind me not to be a doctor, OK?

If I do come for a visit, let's make a music video. What do you think? Send me your ideas.

closing
signature

Your cousin,
Dave

See "Understanding Task, Audience, and Purpose," page 14.

*You may want to write a **business letter** to someone you do not know. You might want to request information, order a product, state an opinion, or register a complaint. When you do, remember that a business letter is more formal than a friendly letter.*

heading

25 Lee Road, Apt. 5B
Sacramento, CA 95816
August 31, 199-

inside address

Tru-Scale Models
Customer Service Dept.
11153 Euclid Avenue
Cleveland, OH 44106

greeting

Dear Tru-Scale Models:

body

I bought a plane kit made by your company. It is Lindbergh's Spirit of St. Louis, Model Number 453A. The decals included in the kit are wrong. The picture on the front of the box shows the right decals. The set that I got must be for a different model.

I have enclosed the incorrect decals. Please send the correct set to the address above. Thank you.

closing

Yours truly,

signature

Maya Hartman

MODEL: ENVELOPE

A letter needs an **envelope**. Even a postcard needs an address. Make sure the post office can read your writing. Proofread the address, too.

return address

mailing address

> Maya Hartman
> 25 Lee Road, Apt. 5B
> Sacramento, CA 95816
>
> Tru-Scale Models
> Customer Service Dept.
> 11153 Euclid Avenue
> Cleveland, OH 44106

You can use the two-letter postal abbreviations for each state. Both letters are capitals. These abbreviations don't use periods.

Alabama AL	Kentucky KY	Ohio OH
Alaska AK	Louisiana LA	Oklahoma OK
Arizona AZ	Maine ME	Oregon OR
Arkansas AR	Maryland MD	Pennsylvania PA
California CA	Massachusetts MA	Rhode Island RI
Colorado CO	Michigan MI	South Carolina SC
Connecticut CT	Minnesota MN	South Dakota SD
Delaware DE	Mississippi MS	Tennessee TN
District of	Missouri MO	Texas TX
Columbia DC	Montana MT	Utah UT
Florida FL	Nebraska NE	Vermont VT
Georgia GA	Nevada NV	Virginia VA
Hawaii HI	New Hampshire NH	Washington WA
Idaho ID	New Jersey NJ	West Virginia WV
Illinois IL	New Mexico NM	Wisconsin WI
Indiana IN	New York NY	Wyoming WY
Iowa IA	North Carolina NC	
Kansas KS	North Dakota ND	

See "Abbreviations," page 156.

A good telephone **message** is complete and easy to read. When you take a message, check to see that you have all the information you need. These hints can help you take messages:

- Include the caller's name, the time of the call, the caller's telephone number, and the specific message.

- Ask the caller to repeat anything you didn't catch. Ask how to spell unfamiliar names, too.

- Repeat the caller's telephone number to make sure you took it down correctly.

- If your first message is sloppy, make a neat copy. Double-check to see that your copy has the right name and phone number.

11:00 Saturday

Dad—
Mrs. Banowsky called to see if you could bring a salad instead of a dessert to the potluck dinner next Fri. Call her at 555-2193 to tell her what you are bringing.
Sasha

MODEL: MESSAGE FORM

*Some businesses and schools use **message form**s to keep track of telephone messages. Fill out a different form for each phone call you take. Find out where to place the messages so that they will be found.*

correct details circled

details written on line
clear abbreviations

Neatness counts!

To *Dr. Metzger*
Date *10/12/9 —*   Time *3:00*   A.M.
(**P.M.**)

WHILE YOU WERE OUT

M *s. Ruiz*
Of *Hawksbridge Elem. School*
Phone *(813) 555-7626*

Telephoned	X	Please call	X
Called to see you		Will call again	
Returned your call		Urgent	

Message *She wants to discuss your visit to speak to her class on Mon., Oct. 20, at 11:00.*
Meg

See "Abbreviations," page 156.

Forms require neat and careful writing. You may need to fill out forms to join clubs, to get a library card, or to buy merchandise from catalogs. Read the form before you start filling it out.

neat printing in pen (not pencil)

information written in correct place

Proofread form for mistakes before mailing.

ORDER FORM
Zippo Novelties
24 Wacky Way
Arlington, IL 60005

Svea Barnett
329 Wigham Rd.
St. Paul, MN 55112

Product Number	Page Number	Product Name	How Many	Cost Each	Total Cost
H137	4	Chattering Teeth	1	$1.95	$1.95
E445	14	Bouncing Penguin	2	$3.50	$7.00
R892	15	Miniature Camera	1	$4.95	$4.95

Subtotal	$13.90
Shipping (see chart below)	$3.50
Total	$17.40

Up to $10	$2.75
$10.01 - $25	$3.50
$25.01 and up	$4.50

WRITING TO LEARN

MODEL: NOTE-TAKING

Note-taking can help you remember what you learn from listening in class or from reading. Notes are helpful when they are organized and easy to read. These hints can help you when you are taking notes:

- **Include important words or phrases.**

- **Define new terms.**

- **Use abbreviations that make sense to you.**

Order of information is logical.

When Golda Meir became prime minister of Israel in 1968, she remembered the difficult times she faced as a child. She was born in Kiev, Russia, on May 3, 1898. Her family was persecuted because they were Jewish. The Meir family finally left Russia and settled in America. In her comfortable home in Milwaukee, Meir dreamed of helping all Jews live in peace.

Notes summarize important details.

Word to check in dictionary

> Golda Meir
> b. in Russia (1898)
> prime minister of Israel (1968)
> first lived in Kiev, then in Milwaukee
> look up: persecuted

See "Writing to Learn—Note Page," page 34, and "Abbreviations," page 156.

*You can write a **summary** to help you remember something you have read or seen. A summary tells about main events or ideas. If you are summarizing a story, tell about the beginning, the middle, and the ending. If you are summarizing nonfiction, tell about the main ideas.*

main events of the story

Minor details left out.

generalization about theme

In *The Wizard of Oz*, Dorothy gets caught in a tornado and wakes up in the weird land of Oz. She meets a scarecrow who wishes for a brain, a tin man who wishes for a heart, and a lion who wishes for courage. When they kill the Wicked Witch of the West, the Wizard grants their wishes. Dorothy almost gets stuck in Oz, but then she wakes up from her dream. Her adventure has taught her that there's no place like home.

See "Editing Wordy Sentences," page 25.

Writing for a Test

Many **tests** have written sections. When you write for a test, you demonstrate special skills. You are usually given a topic and a time limit. The writing process can help you adapt your writing style to meet this challenge.

PREWRITING

Analyzing a Topic

- Do I understand the question?

- Am I being asked to compare, contrast, give an opinion, explain, or describe?

- What form of writing will be most effective?

Gathering Information

- Am I allowed to look in books while I write?

- Would it help to make a rough outline before I write?

D R A F T I N G

- Can I focus my writing by beginning with a clear topic sentence?

- How much time do I have for this assignment?

R E S P O N D I N G   A N D   R E V I S I N G

- Have I answered the question completely?

- Should I add any additional information?

- Are there any incorrect statements that I should change?

P R O O F R E A D I N G

- Have I checked the spelling of every word?

- Have I checked for mistakes in grammar?

P U B L I S H I N G

- Do I have time to make a neater copy?

- If not, are there any sloppy sections I should write on another page?

TIMED WRITING

Think:

Plan — 5 min.

Write — 12 min.

Check — 3 min.

You may face a time limit when you write for a test. Don't panic. You can manage your time well if you plan ahead.

Essay Question B (20 minutes): What changes took place during the Industrial Revolution? Give three examples.

freewrite

2 factories increased
1 family businesses decreased
4 farms got bigger
3 cities grew

organize

topic sentence: The technology of the Industrial Revolution changed American life forever.

write

check

B. The technology of the Industrial Revolution changed American life forever. Family businesses were replaced by big factories. Farming became more automated. Inventions like the cotton gin made large-scale farming more efficient. The Industrial Revolution also led to the growth of cities. As rural jobs disappeared, people came to cities to find jobs in the new factories.

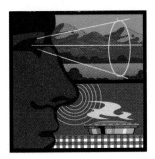

Read: "nose is to smell as eye is to —." Think about the relationship between the first two words.

Hint: Try reading the question *before* you read the passage.

Think: Is my answer complete?

Sometimes a test question will ask you to write a word, a phrase, or a sentence. These questions are called *prompts*. When writing to prompts, read the question carefully. Here are some examples:

Analogy

---

nose : smell :: eye : <u>see</u>

Reading Comprehension

Ellis Island was the main immigration station for the United States between 1892 and 1943. About 17 million people entered America through its gates.

Question: What was Ellis Island's function before 1943?

Ellis Island was the main immigration station for the United States before 1943.

Recall

What is a trapezoid?

A trapezoid is a four-sided shape that has one pair of parallel sides.

PICTURE PROMPT

Some tests will ask you to write about a picture. Plan your time before you write. Take enough time to study the picture carefully.

Write a character sketch. Use your imagination and details from the picture.

Response fits the assignment.

details from the picture

additional details from the writer's imagination

Uncle Raul loves to make up silly songs. He plays beautiful melodies on his guitar and sings whatever comes into his head. One time, he wrote a song about his daughter, Lisa. He had already started when he realized that it was hard to rhyme a word with her name. Thinking quickly, he compared her to a pepperoni pizza. His family members still ask him to sing the "Lisa Pizza" song every year on her birthday.

See "Timed Writing," page 88.

Grammar, Usage, and Mechanics

SENTENCES

A *sentence* is a group of words that expresses a complete thought. A sentence names someone or something. It tells what that person or thing is or does. Begin every sentence with a capital letter, and end it with an end mark. These word groups are sentences:

Many schools today teach foreign languages.

Some students begin a language in high school.

Students in Europe begin in the fourth grade.

These word groups are not sentences. They do not express a complete thought.

in the Russian language

prefer Spanish

by speaking the language

Exercise 1

Tell whether each word group is a sentence or not a sentence.

1. June began to study a foreign language.
2. Begins in the fourth grade.
3. June could choose one of four languages.
4. The languages were French, Spanish, Russian, and German.
5. June and her parents decided on Russian.
6. A native speaker of Russian.
7. At first, June had trouble.
8. Learning a different alphabet was not easy.
9. The shapes of the letters.
10. June learned many Russian words.

For additional practice, turn to pages 166–167.

Writing Application

Work with a partner to write a list of helpful hints for new students. Your list should have at least ten sentences.

SENTENCES

DECLARATIVE SENTENCE

A *declarative sentence* makes a statement. Use a period (.) at the end of a declarative sentence.

The teacher gave the instructions in Spanish.

The young girl listened carefully.

She did not know some of the words.

INTERROGATIVE SENTENCE

An *interrogative sentence* asks a question. Use a question mark (?) at the end of an interrogative sentence.

Who is the author?

Is she a Spanish writer?

Did you enjoy the story?

EXCLAMATORY SENTENCE

An *exclamatory sentence* expresses strong feeling. Use an exclamation point (!) at the end of an exclamatory sentence.

What a wonderful drawing you've made!

The sky is so beautiful!

What vivid colors those are!

Exercise 2

Read each sentence. Tell whether it is declarative or interrogative.

1. I liked this story.
2. The plot was interesting.
3. Where does the story take place?
4. Some of the sentences are quite long.
5. Did you understand all the new words?

Exercise 3

Tell how to begin and end each sentence correctly.

6. what is the name of that book
7. the story is a mystery
8. the author wrote it in Spanish
9. who translated the story
10. can I buy a copy of the book

Writing Application

Create questions and answers for a celebrity interview. Then share your interview.

SENTENCES

IMPERATIVE SENTENCE

An *imperative sentence* gives a command. Use a period (.) at the end of an imperative sentence. The subject of an imperative sentence is *you* (understood).

(you) **Wait a moment.**

(you) **Look at that cloud.**

Exercise 4

Read each sentence. Tell whether it is exclamatory or imperative.

1. Bring me my glasses.
2. What small birds they are!
3. Tell me the name of the bird.

Exercise 5

Tell how to begin and end each sentence correctly.

4. hand that guidebook to me
5. what an unusual name that is
6. take a picture of it

For additional practice, turn to pages 168–169.

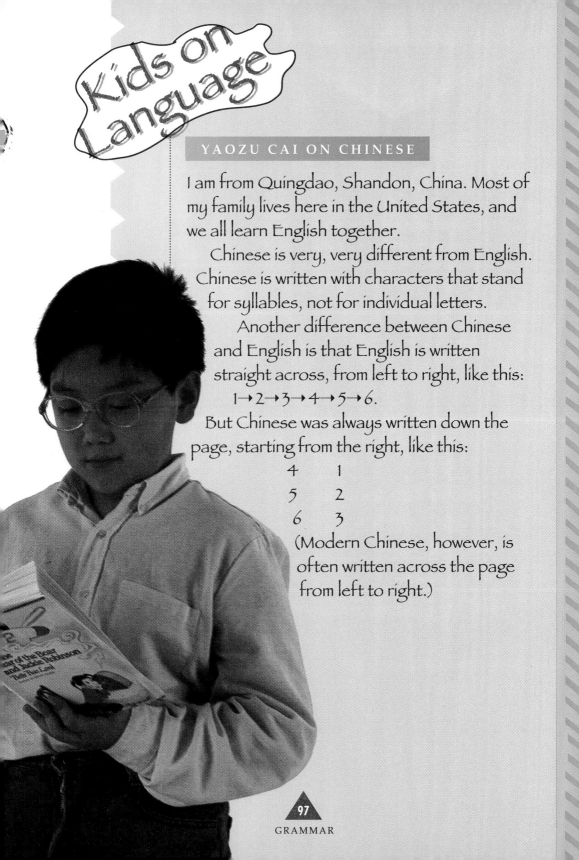

Kids on Language

YAOZU CAI ON CHINESE

I am from Quingdao, Shandon, China. Most of my family lives here in the United States, and we all learn English together.

Chinese is very, very different from English. Chinese is written with characters that stand for syllables, not for individual letters.

Another difference between Chinese and English is that English is written straight across, from left to right, like this:

1→2→3→4→5→6.

But Chinese was always written down the page, starting from the right, like this:

4   1

5   2

6   3

(Modern Chinese, however, is often written across the page from left to right.)

SENTENCES

SUBJECT AND PREDICATE

Every sentence is made up of two parts, a subject and a predicate. The *subject* tells whom or what the sentence is about. The *predicate* tells what the subject is or does.

Subject	Predicate
The hinge	was rusty.
It	squeaked.
Doreen	found an oil can.

Exercise 6

Read each sentence. Tell whether the underlined part is the subject or the predicate of the sentence.

1. <u>Doreen</u> helped her father and mother.
2. The family <u>owned a small farm.</u>
3. Everyone <u>had daily tasks.</u>
4. <u>She</u> tended the chickens.
5. Her brother <u>took care of the cows and pigs.</u>

Exercise 7

Read each sentence. Identify the subject and the predicate.

6. Robbie looked out the window.
7. He sighed with relief.
8. His sister was coming home.
9. Cynthia had fallen on the ice.
10. An ambulance took her to the hospital.
11. The doctor put her leg in a cast.
12. Robbie visited Cynthia every day.
13. Two friends helped her with schoolwork.
14. The hospital released Cynthia.
15. Cynthia was grateful for Robbie's help.

For additional practice, turn to pages 170–171.

Writing Application

Work with a partner to write sentences describing your favorite TV shows. Check that each sentence has a subject and a predicate.

COMPLETE SUBJECT AND SIMPLE SUBJECT

The *complete subject* includes all the words that tell whom or what the sentence is about.

The water from the river rose steadily.

The *simple subject* is the main word or words in the complete subject.

water

Sometimes the simple subject and the complete subject of a sentence are the same.

Bennie could not believe it.

Exercise 8

Read each sentence. The complete subject of each sentence is underlined. Identify the simple subject.

1. **Many homes were flooded by the Mississippi River.**
2. **Heavy sandbags were used for protection against the flood.**
3. **Volunteers of all ages worked on sandbag crews day and night.**
4. **People in towns and cities fought the raging waters.**
5. **Farms along the river were also underwater.**

Exercise 9

Read each sentence. Identify the complete subject and the simple subject.

6. Flora is Marco's little sister.

7. She is learning to answer the telephone.

8. Her brother practices telephone conversations with her.

9. Marco pretends to be a stranger on the telephone.

10. The telephone must not ring more than twice.

11. Little Flora forgets to ask the name of the caller sometimes.

12. A pad of yellow paper is now kept next to the phone.

13. Flora's aunt called yesterday.

14. Her cheerful voice was familiar to Flora.

15. The family has a new secretary now!

For additional practice, turn to pages 172–173.

Writing Application

Brainstorm ideas for a sports report. Write sentences about the sports activity. Underline the complete subject of each sentence.

SENTENCES

COMPLETE PREDICATE AND SIMPLE PREDICATE

The *complete predicate* includes all the words that tell what the subject of the sentence is or does.

The moving van <u>stopped in front of the house.</u>

The *simple predicate* is the main word or words in the complete predicate.

<u>stopped</u>

Exercise 10

Read each sentence. The complete predicate of each sentence is underlined. Identify the simple predicate.

1. The man <u>opened the doors of the truck.</u>
2. Mel's sister Alana <u>watched the movers.</u>
3. They <u>moved the refrigerator into place.</u>
4. Mel <u>helped his father with the rugs.</u>
5. Mother <u>began the unpacking.</u>

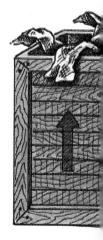

Exercise 11

Read each sentence. Identify the complete predicate and the simple predicate.

6. Many books were still in boxes.
7. Some of the children's clothes and shoes were still packed.
8. Mother unpacked the last of the dishes.
9. Alana found the box with her pencils and paper.
10. She found her schoolbooks with the blankets.
11. Mel discovered his schoolbooks in a suitcase.
12. The two children were ready for school.
13. The family needed groceries.
14. All of them went to a restaurant.
15. The busy day ended with a trip to the supermarket.

For additional practice, turn to pages 174 – 175.

Writing Application

Think of idea sentences for a narrative about an event that takes place at home. Underline the simple predicates in your sentences.

SENTENCES

COMPOUND SUBJECT

A *compound subject* is two or more subjects that have the same predicate. The subjects in a compound subject are usually joined by *and* or *or.*

In each sentence below, the underlined words make up the compound subject.

<u>Mother</u> and <u>Dad</u> are at work.

<u>Jim</u> or <u>I</u> will take Aunt Lydia to the mall.

If there are three or more simple subjects in a compound subject, use commas to separate them.

<u>Horses</u>, <u>cows</u>, and <u>sheep</u> are at the petting zoo.

Exercise 12

Tell which words make up the compound subject. Identify the word that joins the simple subjects.

1. Aunt Lydia and I will buy the groceries.
2. She and Jim often stop by the petting zoo.
3. The deer and the goat are my favorites.
4. The horse, the sheep, and the goat remind Aunt Lydia of her home in Australia.
5. Children and adults enjoy this zoo.

COMPOUND PREDICATE

A *compound predicate* is two or more predicates that have the same subject. The predicates in a compound predicate are usually joined by *and, but,* or *or.*

In each sentence below, the underlined words make up the compound predicate.

Greta <u>sat</u> quietly and <u>looked</u> at her notebook.

She <u>wrote</u> a sentence but <u>erased</u> it.

If there are three or more simple predicates in a compound predicate, use commas to separate them.

Greta now <u>speaks</u>, <u>reads</u>, and <u>writes</u> English.

Exercise 13

Tell which words make up the compound predicate. Identify the word that joins the simple predicates.

6. Hans speaks English but uses German word order.
7. Greta learns quickly and remembers the names of things easily.
8. Their father writes to them in English and expects letters in English from them.
9. Anne takes German and practices with Greta.
10. They read stories, sing songs, or recite poetry together.

For additional practice, turn to pages 176–177.

For additional practice, turn to pages 176–177.

Writing Application

Gather ideas for a description of someone you know. Use one sentence with a compound subject and one with a compound predicate.

SENTENCES

SIMPLE SENTENCE

A sentence that expresses only one complete thought is a *simple sentence.* The subject or predicate in a simple sentence may be simple or compound.

Subject	Predicate
The sky	grew dark.
Rain and hail	fell.
Tree branches	snapped and broke.

COMPOUND SENTENCE

A *compound sentence* is made up of two or more simple sentences joined by a conjunction such as *and, or,* or *but.* Use a comma before the conjunction.

The rain came down hard, and we could not see.

Dad drove slowly, but we did not stop.

CONJUNCTION

A *conjunction* is a word that connects words or groups of words in a sentence. Some common conjunctions are *and, but,* and *or.*

Lightning flashed, and peals of thunder followed.

Many cars pulled off the road, but some cars did not.

Exercise 14

Identify each sentence as a simple sentence or a compound sentence.

1. We couldn't see the lines on the road.
2. Rover was frightened by the thunder and the lightning.
3. Several pieces of hail dented the hood.
4. Dad seemed nervous, but Mom remained calm.

Exercise 15

Identify the conjunction in each compound sentence.

5. The air was humid, and the ground was soaked.
6. We heard thunder in the distance, but the storm was moving away from us.
7. A walk in the rain can be nice, or it can be miserable.
8. Sudden rainstorms are usually heavy, but they do not last long.

For additional practice, turn to pages 178–179.

Writing Application

Collect ideas and images for a nature poem. Use at least two compound sentences in your poem. Share your poem.

NOUNS

NOUN

A *noun* is a word that names a person, a place, a thing, or an idea. Nouns tell *who, what,* and *where.* Using exact nouns will help you paint a clear picture in your writing.

carpenter	rabbit	farm	nail	honesty
uncle	wolf	ocean	cloud	sadness
pilot	cheetah	river	tree	memory
biologist	parrot	park	chair	pleasure
student	oyster	desert	castle	mystery

Exercise 16

Tell whether each underlined word names a person, a place, a thing, or an idea.

1. The snowstorm lasted all day.
2. The snow covered our city.
3. People shoveled their sidewalks.
4. The joy of the children was obvious.
5. We found warmth by the fireplace.
6. Some adults think that a foot of snow is a disaster.
7. Icy roads fill many drivers with fear.
8. Many of the kids in our neighborhood have sleds.
9. We have fun together from early morning until sunset.
10. Then our parents call us to come home for dinner.

Writing Application

Select a noun as the basis of a name poem. Each letter of the noun will begin a line of the poem. Share your poems in a group.

NOUNS

A *common noun* names any person, place, thing or idea.
A common noun begins with a lowercase letter.

singer	church	paper
lawyer	hallway	cup
waiter	restaurant	table
painter	house	window
engineer	station	ticket

Exercise 17

Read each sentence and identify the
common nouns.

1. A storm developed out over the sea.
2. The winds of the hurricane were strong.
3. The house suffered damage.

4. A boy opened his umbrella in the rain.
5. The river overflowed its banks.

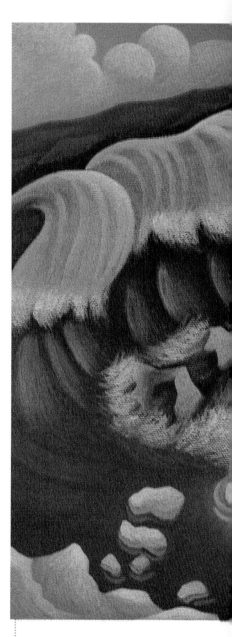

A *proper noun* names a particular person, place, or thing. Begin each important word in a proper noun with a capital letter.

Abraham Lincoln	Illinois	Civil War
Linda Ronstadt	Mexico	Spanish
Janet Reno	Caribbean Sea	Bill of Rights
Winnie the Pooh	Sleepy Hollow	Old Faithful
Uncle Mark	Clark Street	Drake Hotel

Exercise 18

Read each sentence and identify the proper nouns.

6. The cold wind blows down from Canada into the United States.

7. Parts of the Great Lakes freeze over.

8. Harbors on Lake Superior and Lake Huron must be closed.

9. Ships leaving from Duluth and Chicago are idle.

10. The coldest temperatures in the United States are in Alaska.

For additional practice, turn to pages 180 – 181.

Writing Application

Brainstorm ideas for a description of a person, place, or thing you know. Use proper nouns. Share your description.

NOUNS

The names or titles of specific persons, places, and things are proper nouns. Important words in titles are capitalized.

names	**Pamela Ann Dixon**
titles	**Governor Richards**
days, months	**Wednesday, February 14**
holidays	**Independence Day**
place names	**New Orleans, Illinois, Brazil, Antarctica**
geographic areas	**Amazon River, Pacific Ocean**
buildings	**White House, World Trade Center**
organizations	**American Red Cross, United Nations**
monuments	**Washington Monument, Grant's Tomb**
short stories	**"The Ransom of Red Chief"**
poems	**"The Raven"**

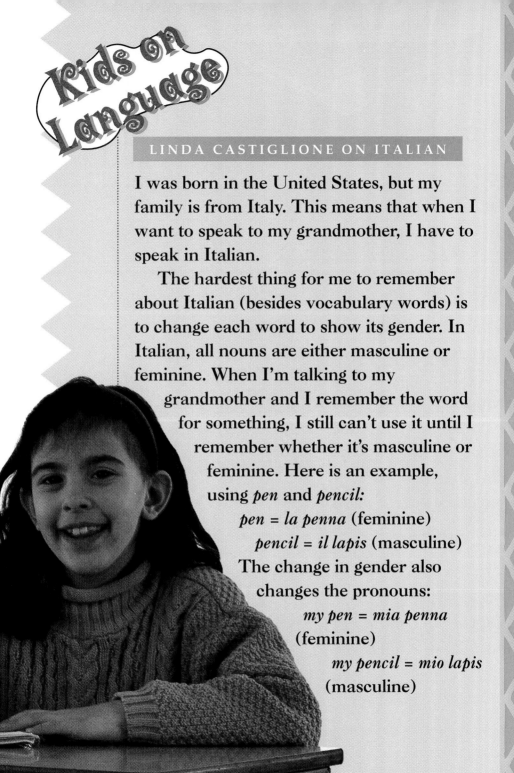

LINDA CASTIGLIONE ON ITALIAN

I was born in the United States, but my family is from Italy. This means that when I want to speak to my grandmother, I have to speak in Italian.

The hardest thing for me to remember about Italian (besides vocabulary words) is to change each word to show its gender. In Italian, all nouns are either masculine or feminine. When I'm talking to my grandmother and I remember the word for something, I still can't use it until I remember whether it's masculine or feminine. Here is an example, using *pen* and *pencil:*

pen = la penna (feminine)
pencil = il lapis (masculine)

The change in gender also changes the pronouns:

my pen = mia penna (feminine)

my pencil = mio lapis (masculine)

NOUNS

SINGULAR NOUN

A *singular noun* names one person, place, thing, or idea.

shirt	stereo	charity	box
town	cello	baby	guess
key	tomato	story	church
safe	hero	lady	bush

PLURAL NOUN

A *plural noun* names more than one person, place, thing, or idea. Make most nouns plural by adding *-s, -es,* or *-ies.* (The *y* at the end of some words changes to *i* before *-es* is added.)

shirts	stereos	charities	boxes
towns	cellos	babies	guesses
keys	tomatoes	stories	churches
safes	heroes	ladies	bushes

Some nouns change spelling for the plural form.

knife, knives	thief, thieves
man, men	mouse, mice
foot, feet	tooth, teeth

Exercise 19

Read each sentence, and tell whether each underlined noun is singular or plural.

1. The castle was set on a <u>hill</u>.
2. The <u>walls</u> were very high.
3. There were very few <u>windows</u>.
4. <u>Thieves</u> could not gain <u>entry</u>.
5. The walls provided a <u>defense</u> against all <u>enemies</u>.

Exercise 20

Give the plural form for each noun.

6. wish
7. scarf
8. video
9. crutch
10. lady
11. toy
12. fox
13. mess
14. pantry
15. child

For additional practice, turn to pages 182–183.

Writing Application

Gather ideas for a news report. Use three singular nouns and three plural nouns. Share your news report.

NOUNS

POSSESSIVE NOUN

A *possessive noun* shows ownership.

the jury	the jury's verdict
the judges	the judges' decisions
the children	the children's toys

SINGULAR POSSESSIVE NOUN

A *singular possessive noun* shows ownership by one person or thing. To form the possessive of most singular nouns, add an apostrophe (') and s.

Peter	Peter's letter
the lawyer	the lawyer's argument
the movie	the movie's plot

Exercise 21

Give the singular possessive form of each noun.

1. the cat
2. the fool
3. the tinsmith
4. the attorney
5. the clerk
6. the raccoon
7. the painter
8. Laura
9. the minister
10. the uncle

PLURAL POSSESSIVE NOUN

A *plural possessive noun* shows ownership by more than one person or thing. To form the possessive of a plural noun that ends in *s*, add an apostrophe (').

the girls	the girls' textbooks
the babies	the babies' gifts
the officers	the officers' uniforms

To form the possessive of a plural noun that does not end in *s*, add an apostrophe (') and *s*.

the women	the women's careers
the mice	the mice's holes
the geese	the geese's nests

Exercise 22
Give the plural possessive form of each noun.

11. the children
12. the horses
13. the Smiths
14. the oxen
15. the women

16. the serfs
17. the puppies
18. the waitresses
19. the members
20. the ladies

Writing Application

Write a narrative telling about an event you remember well. Use two singular and two plural possessive nouns. Share your narrative.

Exercise 23

Tell whether the underlined possessive noun is singular or plural in form.

21. The <u>lawyers'</u> speeches were long.
22. The judge asked for the <u>jurors'</u> attention.
23. A <u>woman's</u> glove became an important clue.
24. The <u>detective's</u> efforts were successful.
25. The report confirmed the <u>witness's</u> words.
26. The attorneys met in the <u>judge's</u> room.
27. The <u>sheriff's</u> deputy brought in a prisoner.
28. The <u>reporters'</u> cameras angered the judge.
29. The <u>jury's</u> verdict was quick.
30. The <u>observers'</u> faces looked stunned.

For additional practice, turn to pages 184–185.

PRONOUNS

PRONOUN

A *pronoun* is a word that takes the place of one or more nouns. Pronouns show number and gender. *Number* tells whether a pronoun is singular or plural. *Gender* tells whether the pronoun is masculine, feminine, or neuter.

John asked Maria when *she* was leaving.

ANTECEDENT

The *antecedent* of a pronoun is the noun or nouns to which the pronoun refers. A pronoun should agree with its antecedent in number and gender.

John saw two *movies* and enjoyed both of *them*.

Exercise 24

Identify the antecedent of each underlined pronoun.

1. Two people missed the flight because <u>they</u> were late.

2. Maria and I enjoyed the dinner <u>we</u> were served.

3. John and I were so hungry that the steward gave <u>us</u> each two desserts.

For additional practice, turn to pages 186–187.

For additional practice, turn to pages 186–187.

Writing Application

Think of ideas for a letter about a trip. Use singular and plural pronouns in your letter. Share your letter.

PRONOUNS

SUBJECT PRONOUN

A *subject pronoun* takes the place of a noun or nouns in the subject of a sentence. *I, you, he, she, it, we,* and *they* are subject pronouns.

We are learning about Benjamin Franklin.
(subject)

He wrote a book called <u>Poor Richard's Almanack</u>.
(subject)

A subject pronoun is often combined with a verb to form a *contraction.* In a contraction, a letter or letters in the verb are dropped and replaced with an apostrophe. Here are some common pronoun-verb contractions.

I'm (I am)	you're (you are)	she's (she is)
I'll (I will)	you'll (you will)	she'll (she will)
I've (I have)	you've (you have)	she's (she has)
we're (we are)	it's (it is)	they're (they are)
we'll (we will)		they'll (they will)
we've (we have)		they've (they have)

You'll enjoy this book.
I've just finished it.
It's about life in the colonies.

OBJECT PRONOUN

An **object pronoun** takes the place of a noun that follows an action verb, such as *see* or *tell*, or a preposition, such as *about, at, by, from, to,* or *with*. The words *me, you, him, her, it, us,* and *them* are object pronouns.

Martha recognized *him* in the photograph.

She showed *us* pictures of Williamsburg.

Al went with *me* to see the colonial exhibit at the museum.

I just heard about *it* last week.

REFLEXIVE PRONOUN

A **reflexive pronoun** refers to the subject of a sentence. The words *myself, yourself, himself, herself,* and *itself* are singular reflexive pronouns.

I observed for *myself* the tower of Old North Church.

Martha bought *herself* a map.

Ourselves, yourselves, and *themselves* are plural reflexive pronouns.

We treated *ourselves* to a tour of historic Boston.

The colonists defended *themselves* against the British.

Writing Application

Brainstorm a list of subject, object, and reflexive pronouns. Use them in a story about a visit. Share your story.

PRONOUNS

A *possessive pronoun* shows ownership and takes the place of a possessive noun. There are two kinds of possessive pronouns. One kind is used before a noun. These pronouns are *my, your, his, her, its, our,* and *their.*

The young soldier loaded *his* musket.

The colonists defended *their* farms.

Our government has *its* roots in the love of freedom.

The second type of possessive pronoun stands alone. These pronouns are *mine, yours, his, hers, ours,* and *theirs.*

Gena is still finishing her report, but I turned *mine* in.

Hers will probably be longer than *yours.*

Exercise 25

Tell whether each underlined word is a *subject, object, reflexive,* or *possessive* pronoun.

1. The Pilgrims left <u>their</u> homes in Europe.

2. Ten weeks later, <u>they</u> landed at Plymouth.

3. Religious reasons brought <u>them</u> to America.

4. The Puritans built <u>their</u> settlement at Salem.

5. The Puritans did all the work by <u>themselves</u>.

For additional practice, turn to pages 188–193.

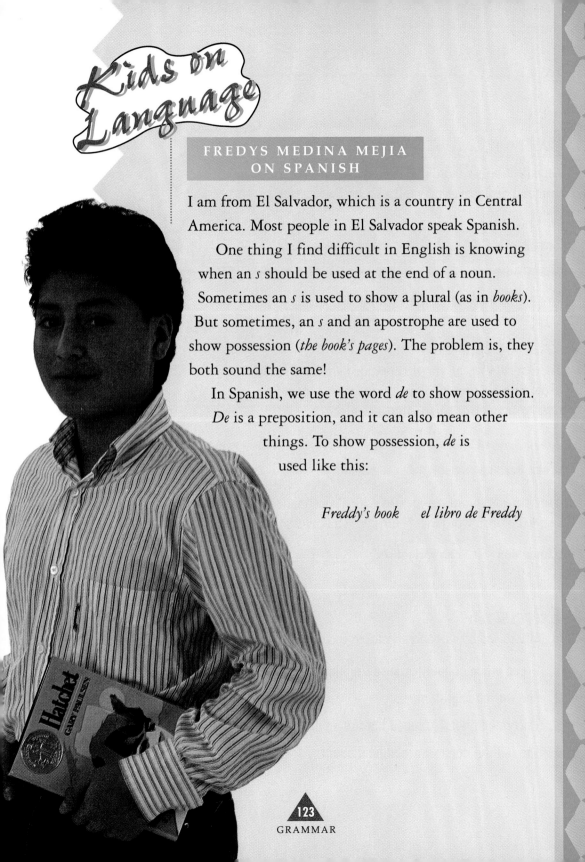

Kids on Language

FREDYS MEDINA MEJIA ON SPANISH

I am from El Salvador, which is a country in Central America. Most people in El Salvador speak Spanish.

One thing I find difficult in English is knowing when an *s* should be used at the end of a noun. Sometimes an *s* is used to show a plural (as in *books*). But sometimes, an *s* and an apostrophe are used to show possession (*the book's pages*). The problem is, they both sound the same!

In Spanish, we use the word *de* to show possession. *De* is a preposition, and it can also mean other things. To show possession, *de* is used like this:

Freddy's book   *el libro de Freddy*

ADJECTIVES

ADJECTIVE

An *adjective* is a word that describes a noun or a pronoun. Adjectives may tell *what kind, how many,* or *which one.*

Grandmother was a *fearless* woman. *(what kind)*

She killed *two* rattlesnakes in a year. *(how many)*

The *second* snake almost bit her. *(which one)*

ARTICLE

The adjectives *a, an,* and *the* are called *articles. The* refers to a particular person, place, thing, or idea. *A* and *an* refer to any person, place, thing, or idea.

***The* farmhouse was at *the* top of *a* hill.**

***A* lilac bush and *an* oak tree grew nearby.**

Use *a* before a word that begins with a consonant sound. Use *an* before a word that begins with a vowel sound.

***a* large dog**   ***an* ancient rock**

Exercise 26

Identify the adjectives and articles in each sentence.

1. I read a book about Florence Nightingale.

2. She was an English nurse.

3. Thirty-eight nurses tended the sick soldiers.

4. The faithful nurses worked long hours.

PROPER ADJECTIVE

A *proper adjective* is formed from a proper noun.
Always capitalize proper adjectives.

French pastry	**Korean** art	**Japanese** tea
Irish song	**American** flag	**Chinese** border
Egyptian citizen	**Canadian** industry	

Exercise 27

Identify the proper adjective in each sentence. Then
name the proper noun from which it is formed.

5. The train winds through the French section of the Alps.

6. The trip ended just across the Swiss border.

7. The American tourists wanted to see Florence, Italy.

8. Florence is famous for masterpieces of Italian art.

9. It is also the birthplace of a famous English woman,
   Florence Nightingale.

For additional practice, turn to pages 194–195.

Writing
Application

Think of a

person you

know and like.

Make a web of

adjectives that

describe that

person. Then

write a sketch

of the person.

ADJECTIVES

COMPARING WITH ADJECTIVES

Adjectives can be used to compare people, places, things, or ideas.

-er and -est

Add -er to most adjectives to compare two things. Add -est to most adjectives to compare more than two things.

The statue in the hall is *old*.

This statue is *older* than that one.

The statue over there is the *oldest* one in the hall.

more and most

More and *most* are used with many adjectives of two or more syllables. When comparing two things, use *more*. When comparing three or more things, use *most*. The word *the* often comes before *most*.

That painting is *valuable*.

This painting is *more valuable* than that one.

The painting over there is *the most valuable* of all.

Exercise 28

Choose the correct comparison form of the adjective in parentheses ( ).

1. My mother's diary is the (old) book in our house.

2. It is (long) than my diary.

Exercise 29

Use *more* or *most* to complete each comparison.

3. Travel by sea was _____ dangerous than by land.
4. Even the _____ careful sailors slipped on the decks.
5. The _____ amazing thing was that no one fell.

Some adjectives have special forms for comparing.

Adjective	Comparing Two	Comparing Three or More
good	better	best
bad	worse	worst

The weather is *better* today than yesterday.

The *best* view is from there.

Our crops look *worse* than yours.

The *worst* drought happened when I was fourteen.

Exercise 30

Complete the sentence by choosing the correct comparison form of the adjective in parentheses ( ).

6. Which of these three quilts has the (good) design?
7. The design in the first is (good) than the design in the second.
8. The stitching in the second quilt is (bad) than the stitching in the first.

For additional practice, turn to pages 196–199.

Writing Application

Use adjectives that show comparison in a paragraph that describes things in your home. Share your writing.

VERBS

A *verb* expresses action or being. The main word in the predicate of a sentence is a verb.

Maya *writes* a wonderful letter.
> *The verb* writes *expresses action.*

Your letters *are* full of news.
> *The verb* are *expresses being.*

Exercise 31

Identify the verb in each sentence.

1. This letter tells about a trip by stagecoach.

2. The handwriting is clear.

3. The writer is a woman.

4. She tells of the dangers of the trip.

5. Stagecoaches carried gold.

6. Bandits robbed some stagecoaches.

7. The woman's trip was a safe one.

8. She traveled west from Missouri to Kansas.

9. That is not a long trip today.

10. Her descriptions are quite vivid.

ACTION VERB

An *action verb* is a word that tells what the subject does, did, or will do.

Letters usually *contain* facts about the writer.

In the past, people *wrote* letters frequently.

I *will mail* your letter this afternoon.

Exercise 32

Identify the action verb in each sentence.

11. I like history.
12. I will study history in college.
13. Novels breathe life into history.
14. You learn about characters through their stories.
15. You will find many stories in private letters.
16. People made copies of their letters.
17. They saved letters from other people.
18. Some people packed trunks full of letters.
19. The letters provide many details of daily life.
20. These letters will fascinate readers for centuries.

Writing Application

Brainstorm ideas for a letter from the past. Use action verbs to tell about events. Share your letter.

VERBS

A *linking verb* connects the subject to a noun or an adjective that names or describes it. The most common linking verbs are forms of *be*, including *am, is, are, was,* and *were*.

Washington Irving *was* a writer.
   (subject)   *(noun)*

His stories *are* still popular.
  (subject)   *(adjective)*

Some other common linking verbs are *appear, become, feel, grow, look, seem,* and *taste*.

The valley *appears* misty.

The Hudson River *looks* beautiful.

The story *seems* familiar.

Exercise 33

Identify the linking verb in each sentence.

1. The main character is Rip Van Winkle.
2. The story became a classic.
3. The time of the story is the colonial period.
4. The colonies become independent of England.
5. Rip grows old during his twenty-year sleep.

For additional practice, turn to pages 200 – 201.

MAIN VERB

A simple predicate may be made up of two or more verbs. The *main verb* is the most important verb in the predicate.

I am *writing* a report about insects.

Insects have *lived* on the earth for more than 400 million years.

You will *enjoy* this book about insects.

Did you *read* the first chapter yet?

Exercise 34

Identify the main verb in each sentence.

6. Do you see that insect?

7. They call it a "monarch butterfly."

8. Insects do not have lungs.

9. Insects exist in every part of the earth.

10. People have thought of insects as harmful.

Create idea sentences for a report on insects. Find the main verbs in your sentences. Share your report.

VERBS

A *helping verb* can work with the main verb to tell about an action. These words are often used as helping verbs:

am	is	has	do	could
was	were	have	does	would
are	will	had	did	should

I *am* watching that anthill.

The ants *have* built a very large hill.

They *will* destroy that leaf.

We *should* check under that log.

Sometimes other words appear between the helping verb and the main verb.

You will *soon* see the ants.

I have *never* seen the queen.

I do *not* believe my eyes.

Did *you* see that anthill?

Exercise 35

Identify the helping verb and the main verb in each sentence.

1. Many fruits and vegetables are pollinated only by insects.
2. Honey, shellac, and silk are produced by insects.
3. Insects have developed a strong sense of taste.
4. Most insects do not use their mouths for taste.
5. Tasters are found on the antennae or the feet.
6. Do you know about the ears of insects?
7. Most insects do not have ears as such.
8. An insect's ears are never found in the insect's head.
9. The ears of crickets are located on their legs.
10. Very high sounds and very low sounds are easily heard by insects.

For additional practice, turn to pages 202–203.

Writing Application

Imagine you are an insect. Tell what you observe. Find the helping verbs and main verbs in your sentences. Share your description.

VERBS

TENSE

The *tense* of a verb shows when the action happens.

There are three basic verb tenses:

I *am taking* a photo of a grasshopper. PRESENT

I *develop* my pictures in my darkroom. PRESENT

I *watched* the grasshopper for an hour. PAST

I *will show* you the photographs tomorrow. FUTURE

Exercise 36

Tell whether the verb in each sentence is in the present tense, in the past tense, or in the future tense.

1. My new camera takes great color pictures.

2. I used it for my insect photographs.

3. They will be on exhibit next week.

4. Four people will judge the exhibit.

5. Some of my pictures are in black and white.

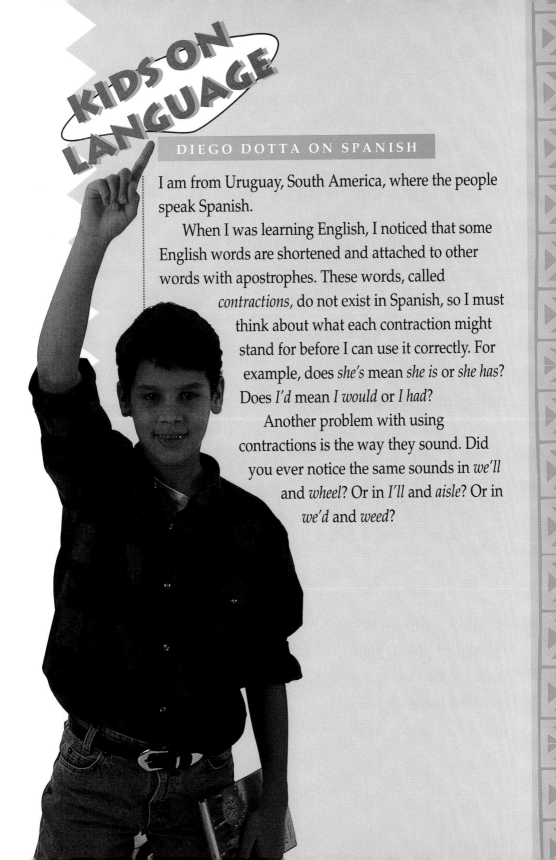

KIDS ON LANGUAGE

DIEGO DOTTA ON SPANISH

I am from Uruguay, South America, where the people speak Spanish.

When I was learning English, I noticed that some English words are shortened and attached to other words with apostrophes. These words, called *contractions*, do not exist in Spanish, so I must think about what each contraction might stand for before I can use it correctly. For example, does *she's* mean *she is* or *she has*? Does *I'd* mean *I would* or *I had*?

Another problem with using contractions is the way they sound. Did you ever notice the same sounds in *we'll* and *wheel*? Or in *I'll* and *aisle*? Or in *we'd* and *weed*?

VERBS

PRESENT TENSE

A verb in the *present tense* shows action that happens now or action that happens over and over.

Use these rules for spelling singular present-tense verbs when the subject is a singular noun or *he, she,* or *it:*

Add -*s* to most verbs.

walk—walks   **sit—sits**

Add -*es* to verbs ending in *s, ch, sh, x,* or *z.*

miss—misses   **catch—catches**   **wish—wishes**
mix—mixes   **buzz—buzzes**

If the verb ends in a consonant plus *y,* change the *y* to *i* and add -*es.*

dry—dries   **fly—flies**

Exercise 37

Give the present-tense form of the verb in parentheses ( ) that completes the sentence correctly.

1. Sandy (stop) by my house almost every night.
2. She (help) me with my project.
3. She (watch) me work.
4. Sandy often (lend) me books.
5. I (carry) them back to the library.

A verb in the *past tense* shows action that happened in the past.

Use these rules for spelling past-tense verbs:

Add -*ed* to most verbs.

look—looked   **roll—rolled**

If a verb ends in *e*, add -*d*.

use—used   **move—moved**

If a verb ends with a consonant plus *y*, change the *y* to *i* and add -*ed*.

try—tried   **empty—emptied**

If a verb ends with consonant-vowel-consonant, double the final consonant and add -*ed*.

dip—dipped   **shop—shopped**

Exercise 38

Write the past-tense form of the verb in parentheses ( ) that completes the sentence correctly.

6. Yesterday I (spill) paint on my jeans.

7. I (wash) it off immediately.

8. The paint (dry) on the brushes.

9. I quickly (cover) the paint cans.

10. I almost (drop) my painting.

Writing Application

Create a poem about the sky. Use verbs in both the present tense and the past tense. Share your poem.

VERBS

An *irregular verb* is a verb that does not end with *-ed* in the past tense. This chart shows some irregular verbs.

Verb	Present	Past	Past with Helping Verb
be	am, is, are	was, were	(has, have, had) been
begin	begin(s)	began	(has, have, had) begun
bring	bring(s)	brought	(has, have, had) brought
come	come(s)	came	(has, have, had) come
do	do(es)	did	(has, have, had) done
give	give(s)	gave	(has, have, had) given
have	have, has	had	(has, have, had) had
make	make(s)	made	(has, have, had) made
say	say(s)	said	(has, have, had) said
see	see(s)	saw	(has, have, had) seen
sing	sing(s)	sang	(has, have, had) sung
write	write(s)	wrote	(has, have, had) written

Exercise 39

Supply the past-tense form of the verb in parentheses ( ) that completes the sentence.

1. Last night we (give) our final performance.
2. The choir (sing) better than ever before.
3. The audience (begin) cheering at the end.
4. We all (have) tears in our eyes.

FUTURE TENSE

A verb in the *future tense* shows action that will happen in the future. To form the future tense of a verb, use the helping verb *will* with the main verb.

The audience **will have** a surprise in store.

The musicians **will play** bells.

Exercise 40

Give the future-tense form of the verb in parentheses ( ).

5. Members of Congress (attend) a concert.
6. The players (be) guests at a reception.
7. The concert (produce) funds for charity.

For additional practice, turn to pages 204–213.

For additional practice, turn to pages 204–213.

Writing Application

Write a narrative about a special moment. Use past-tense verbs in your writing. Share your narrative.

ADVERBS

ADVERB

An *adverb* is a word that describes a verb, an adjective, or another adverb. An adverb tells *how, when, where,* or *to what extent.*

Desert flowers bloom *quickly.*
 (tells how)

The desert is beautiful *now.*
 (tells when)

Plants are flowering *there.*
 (tells where)

The desert is *very* dry.*
 (tells to what extent)

Many adverbs that tell *how* end in *-ly.*

Exercise 41

Identify the adverb that describes each underlined word. Then tell whether the adverb tells *how, when, where,* or *to what extent.*

1. The temperature was very <u>high</u>.
2. The sun <u>beat</u> down on the land.
3. An unusually <u>large</u> snake came into view.
4. The snake moved too <u>swiftly</u> for us to identify it.
5. A few birds <u>sat</u> quietly on sagebrush plants.
6. The car drove very <u>slowly</u> down the highway.
7. We suddenly <u>spied</u> a building ahead.
8. We were then <u>disappointed</u>.
9. The hot-air currents had cleverly <u>created</u> a mirage.
10. The building soon <u>disappeared</u> into thin air.

For additional practice, turn to pages 214–215.

For additional practice, turn to pages 214–215.

Writing Application

Think of details for a narrative about a journey. Use adverbs to make your writing clear. Share your narrative.

ADVERBS

COMPARISON WITH ADVERBS

Adverbs can be used to compare two or more actions.

When you compare two actions, add *-er* to most short adverbs. When you compare more than two actions, add *-est* to most short adverbs.

soon, sooner, soonest   deep, deeper, deepest

Autumn comes *sooner* in Maine than in Virginia.

The snow was the *deepest* I had ever seen.

Use *more* and *most* before most adverbs that have two or more syllables. When you compare two actions, use *more*. When you compare more than two, use *most*.

You must drive *more carefully* in wet weather than in dry weather.

Plows clear the roads *most frequently* on holidays.

The adverbs *well* and *badly* have special forms of comparison.

Adverb	To Compare Two	More Than Two
well	better	best
badly	worse	worst

This snowblower works *better* with dry snow than with wet snow.

It works *best* on new snow.

It works *worst* in high drifts.

Exercise 42

Give the comparative form of the adverb in parentheses ( ) that correctly completes the sentence.

1. The winter will arrive (soon) than usual.
2. People eat soup (hungrily) on cold days than on warm ones.
3. Of all the winter months, January is the one when Jack Frost paints the windows (beautifully).
4. The snow drifts (deep) of all on the north side of the house.
5. In wet weather, cars skid (easily) than trucks.

Exercise 43

Complete each sentence with the form of *well* or *badly* that makes sense.

6. She drives (well) than I do.
7. This car takes curves (well) of all the cars I know of.
8. I drive (badly) on city streets than on highways.
9. He skied (badly) on Sunday than on Saturday.
10. I skate (badly) of all on mushy ice.

For additional practice, turn to pages 216–217.

For additional practice, turn to pages 216–217.

Writing Application

Brainstorm ideas for a description of a very cold or a very hot day. Use adverb comparisons in your writing. Share your description.

NEGATIVES

NEGATIVE

A word that means "no" or "not" is called a *negative*.

The words *never, no, nobody, none, not, nothing,* and *nowhere* are common negatives.

This pear is *not* ripe.

Contractions can be made with negatives.

The market *wasn't* (was not) open.

Use only one negative in a sentence.

INCORRECT: **We *never* have *no* strawberries.**

CORRECT: **We *never* have any strawberries.**

Exercise 44

Select the word in parentheses ( ) that correctly completes the sentence. Avoid double negatives.

1. My friends haven't (ever, never) picked strawberries.

2. We didn't find (any, no) bugs on them.

3. Haven't you (ever, never) had strawberries and cream?

4. Nothing (would, wouldn't) please me more.

5. I can't think of (anything, nothing) better.

For additional practice, turn to pages 218–219.

PREPOSITIONS

PREPOSITION

A *preposition* is a word that shows the relationship of a noun or pronoun to another word in the sentence.

There are three eggs *in* the robin's nest.

You can see them *from* the porch.

Common Prepositions

above	between	in	on	toward
after	by	inside	onto	under
around	down	into	out	until
at	during	near	over	up
before	for	of	through	with
behind	from	off	to	without

Exercise 45

Identify the preposition in each sentence.

1. The robins always build a nest in that tree.
2. We have a birdhouse hanging from a branch.
3. Do you have a birdbath for the birds?
4. The feeder is full of seeds.
5. Can you see the woodpecker on the tree trunk?

PREPOSITIONS

OBJECT OF THE PREPOSITION

The noun or pronoun that follows a preposition is the *object of the preposition.*

The oak is the oldest tree in *town.*

The citizens built a fence around *it.*

A preposition may have more than one object.

We pitched the tent between an *oak* and an *elm.*

Exercise 46

The underlined word in each sentence is the object of a preposition. Identify the preposition for each object.

1. Sketch that tree in your <u>notebook</u>.

2. Copy your sketch onto white <u>paper</u>.

3. Draw the branches with graceful <u>curves</u>.

4. What colors shall I use for the <u>leaves</u>?

5. Your drawing will look larger inside a <u>frame</u>.

PREPOSITIONAL PHRASE

A *prepositional phrase* is made up of a preposition, the object of the preposition, and all the words in between.

The tree *with red leaves* is a Japanese maple.

We have many kinds *of trees* here.

We once built a tree house *in that cherry tree.*

Exercise 47

Find the prepositional phrases. Identify each preposition.

6. Plants and trees are important for the earth.

7. They take carbon dioxide from the air.

8. Then they change it into oxygen.

9. Carbon dioxide comes from animals and humans.

10. The production of it is absolutely essential.

For additional practice, turn to pages 220–221.

Writing Application

Think of possible first lines for a speech that include prepositional phrases. Exchange your first lines with a partner.

USAGE

Troublesome Words

TO, TOO, TWO

Use *to* to mean "in the direction of."

Are you going *to* town?

Use *too* to mean "also" or "very."

May I come, *too*?

You are *too* kind.

Use *two* to mean the number 2.

We have room for just *two* more.

GOOD, WELL

The word *good* is an adjective that describes a noun.

That bread tastes *good*.

The word *well* can be an adjective or an adverb.

Use *well* as an adjective when you mean "healthy."

After being sick, I am *well* again.

Use *well* as an adverb to tell how something is done.

Are you doing *well* in school?

THEIR, THERE, THEY'RE

Use *their* when you mean "belonging to them."

***Their* house is only a block away.**

Use *there* to indicate where something is or to introduce a verb.

We left our coats *there*.

***There* are two shows today.**

Use *they're* as a contraction for *they are*.

***They're* my cousins.**

ITS, IT'S

Use *its* when you mean "belonging to it."

The puppy keeps chasing *its* tail.

Use *it's* as a contraction for "it is."

***It's* a cocker spaniel.**

Use **your** when you mean "belonging to you."

Is this *your* jacket?

Use **you're** as a contraction for "you are."

***You're* here just in time.**

Exercise 48

Choose the word in parentheses ( ) that correctly completes each sentence.

1. (Your, You're) just the person I'm looking for.
2. Are you going (to, too, two) the game?
3. (Its, It's) going to start at seven o'clock.
4. Will they be taking (there, their, they're) car?
5. Do you skate, (too, two, to)?
6. Where did you ever learn to ski so (good, well)?
7. Did (your, you're) brother teach you?
8. The ski lodge is over (their, they're, there).
9. (It's, Its) hot chocolate is the best.
10. Hot chocolate is (well, good) at night.

For additional practice, turn to pages 222 – 225.

USAGE

Common Errors

Everyone who uses English uses it incorrectly at times. This incorrect usage is sometimes deliberate, as when people speak or write in slang or informal English. On other occasions, speakers and writers commit some of the following common errors.

SUBJECT-VERB AGREEMENT

Use the *singular* form of a verb with a *singular* subject. Use the *plural* form of a verb with a *plural* subject.

It *doesn't* matter to me.

> NOT:
> **It *don't* matter to me.**

Kids *don't* have to pay.

> NOT:
> **Kids *doesn't* have to pay.**

Sometimes a prepositional phrase comes between the subject and verb of a sentence. Be sure the verb agrees with the subject of the sentence and not the object of the preposition.

Two tires on the car *are* flat.

> NOT:
> **Two tires on the car is flat.**

I, ME

Use *I* as the subject of a sentence.

Carlos and *I* will meet you there.

> NOT:
> **Carlos and me will meet you there.**

Use *me* as an object.

Lisa joined Carlos and *me*.

> NOT:
> **Lisa joined Carlos and I.**

These seats are for you and *me*.

> NOT:
> **These seats are for you and I.**

When referring to yourself and someone else, refer to yourself last.

Sit here with *Lisa* and me.

> NOT:
> **Sit here with me and Lisa.**

Be is one of the most commonly misused verbs in English. Forms of *be* appear very frequently, both as main verbs and as helping verbs. However, *be* by itself very rarely appears as a main verb, except in an imperative sentence (when the subject is understood to be *you*).

Be prepared.

Be ready at six o'clock.

Be proud of your accomplishments.

The rest of the time, *be* takes other forms. The following chart shows the correct forms of *be* to use in most present-tense and past-tense situations.

INFINITIVE: TO BE

	present	past
Singular		
I	am	was
you	are	were
he, she, it, or singular noun	is	was
Plural		
we, you, they, or plural noun	are	were

PUNCTUATION

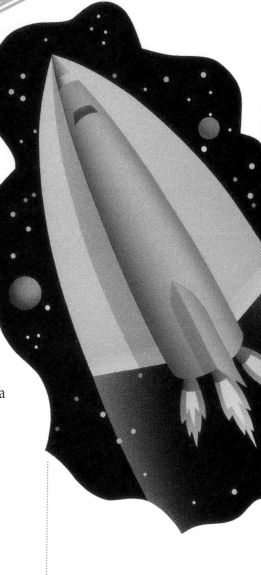

COMMA

A *comma* (*,*) is used to separate one part of a sentence from another to make the meaning clear.

Use a comma to set off such words as *yes*, *no*, and *well* when they begin a sentence.

No, I didn't see the spacecraft land.

Use a comma to set off the name of the person who is spoken to directly in a sentence.

Come here, Alfred, and look at this star.

Cindy, that is the North Star.

Use a comma after each item except the last one in a series of three or more items.

These are pictures of the planets Venus, Mercury, and Jupiter.

Exercise 49

Tell where commas are needed in the following sentences.

1. I am reading about moons asteroids and comets.
2. Alice have you ever seen Andromeda?
3. Yes that is one of the moons of Jupiter.
4. Show me Franco where to look.
5. Gemini Perseus and Orion are three constellations.

For additional practice, turn to pages 226 – 229.

DIALOGUE

Use quotation marks before and after someone's exact words.

Benny asked, "Where is the telescope?"

"It's over here," said Gwen.

If the quotation is interrupted by other words, place quotation marks around the quoted words only.

"Well," said Julio, "I can't see Saturn."

"It's over there," said Mandy. "Look to the left."

Exercise 50

Tell where quotation marks are needed in the following sentences.

1. When did the Russians put *Sputnik* in space? asked Mr. Lopez.

2. Miko answered, I think it was October 4, 1957.

3. Yes, it was very small, said Duane. It weighed only 184 pounds.

4. The first U.S. satellite didn't orbit until January 31, 1958, said Raoul.

5. That's right, said Mr. Lopez. It was called *Explorer I*.

For additional practice, turn to pages 230–231.

Writing Application

Brainstorm ideas for a dialogue about a space voyage. Be sure to use quotation marks correctly. Share your dialogue.

TITLES

TITLES

Capitalize the first word, the last word, and all the important words in a *title*.

<u>The Kid in the Red Jacket</u>

Use quotation marks around the titles of stories, magazine articles, essays, songs, and poems.

"The Last Leaf" (story)
"America the Beautiful" (song)

Underline the titles of books, movies, and television programs and the names of newspapers and magazines.

<u>The Secret Garden</u> (book)
<u>Family Double Dare</u> (television show)

Exercise 51

Tell how the titles in the following sentences should be written.

1. We just received the latest newsweek.
2. The three books listed were storms, hatchet, and many moons.
3. The article endangered species is featured in national geographic.
4. Did you ever see a movie called planet X?

For additional practice, turn to pages 232–233.

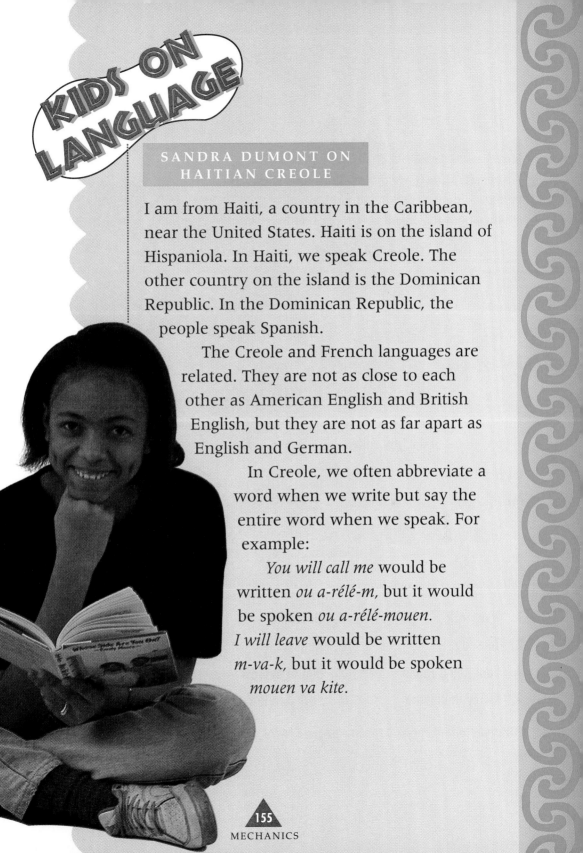

KIDS ON LANGUAGE

I am from Haiti, a country in the Caribbean, near the United States. Haiti is on the island of Hispaniola. In Haiti, we speak Creole. The other country on the island is the Dominican Republic. In the Dominican Republic, the people speak Spanish.

The Creole and French languages are related. They are not as close to each other as American English and British English, but they are not as far apart as English and German.

In Creole, we often abbreviate a word when we write but say the entire word when we speak. For example:

You will call me would be written *ou a-rélé-m*, but it would be spoken *ou a-rélé-mouen*.

I will leave would be written *m-va-k*, but it would be spoken *mouen va kite*.

ABBREVIATIONS

An *abbreviation* is a shortened form of a word. Use periods with most abbreviations. Capitalize abbreviations that stand for proper nouns.

Common Abbreviations

Days	Mon. (Monday)	Fri. (Friday)
Months	Jan. (January)	Oct. (October)
Titles	Dr. (Doctor)	Gov. (Governor)
Addresses	St. (Street)	Ave. (Avenue)
	Rd. (Road)	Blvd. (Boulevard)

You do not need to use periods when writing postal abbreviations of the fifty states.

CA (California)	FL (Florida)
ME (Maine)	IL (Illinois)

Exercise 52
Tell the correct abbreviation.

1. New York
2. Tuesday
3. Paul Kelly, Junior
4. Mercy Boulevard
5. December
6. August
7. Mount Everest
8. Fifth Avenue

For additional practice, turn to pages 234–235.

Handwriting

Handwriting

Handwriting Tips

Using correct posture, writing grip, and paper position can help you write clearly. These tips will help you get ready for writing. See pages 159–164 for tips to help you form letters and words.

Posture

- Sit up straight, with both feet on the floor. Your hips should be toward the back of the chair. Lean forward slightly, but don't slouch.

Paper Position

- Slant the paper toward the elbow of your writing arm. Hold the top corner of the paper with your other hand.

Writing Grip

- Hold your pen or pencil about an inch from the point. Hold it between your thumb and pointer finger. Rest it on your middle finger. Let your other fingers curve under.

Left-hander

Right-hander

HANDWRITING

A B C D E F G H I J
K L M N O P Q R S T
U V W X Y Z

A B C D E F G H I J
K L M N O P Q R S T
U V W X Y Z

a b c d e f g h i j k l m
n o p q r s t u v w x y z

a b c d e f g h i j k l m
n o p q r s t u v w x y z

A B C D E F G H I
J K L M N O P Q R
S T U V W X Y Z

A B C D E F G H I
J K L M N O P Q R
S T U V W X Y Z

a b c d e f g h i
j k l m n o p q r
s t u v w x y z

a b c d e f g h i
j k l m n o p q r
s t u v w x y z

Elements of Handwriting

Shape

Letters must be shaped correctly to make your writing readable.
Write each letter using the correct shape.

correct

radio

incorrect

radio

Spacing of Letters

The letters in a word should not be too close together or too far apart.
Spaces between words and sentences must be even. Remember to leave
room for one spacer ☐ between words and sentences.

correct

Who is it?

incorrect

Who is it?

When space is limited, you may need to write smaller. Keep the
proportions the same as you adjust all the letters in a word and
the spaces between words.

Position

As you write, make the bottom parts of the uppercase and lowercase
letters sit evenly on the bottom line.

correct

St. Louis

incorrect

St. Louis

Elements of Handwriting

Size and Proportion

Each letter should be the correct size. Letters and letter parts should be the same in relation to other letters. Tall letters touch both the top line and the bottom line. Most short letters touch the imaginary midline and the bottom line.

correct

grip

incorrect

grip

When it becomes necessary to write smaller than you usually do, reduce the size of the letters, but keep the proportions the same. Keep all tall letters the same height, all short letters the same height, and all tails the same length.

Slant

To make your writing neat and legible, slant all your letters in the same direction. Keep your paper in the proper position, and hold your pen correctly.

correct

fiddle

incorrect

fiddle

Stroke

All your strokes should be smooth and flowing. Letters and joining strokes should be smooth and even.

correct

bit

unsteady

bit

too light

bit

too dark

bit

Common Errors—Cursive Letters

incorrect

correct

Keep the joining stroke high.
The letters **wa** could look like **uia**.

incorrect

correct

Keep the joining stroke high. Do not loop. The letters **ve** could look like **ree**.

incorrect

correct

Keep the joining stroke high.
The letters **oi** could look like **ai**.

incorrect

correct

Curve your undercurve stroke and slant the down strokes. The **w** could look like **iv**.

incorrect

correct

Be sure the loop moves toward the stem. The **k** could look like **h**.

incorrect

correct

Make the loop at the top and the bottom. The **f** could look like **j**.

HANDWRITING

incorrect   correct

Close the letter **d**. Be sure not to loop. The **d** could look like **cl**.

incorrect   correct

Be sure to retrace. Do not put a loop in the **d**. The letters **od** could look like **oel**.

incorrect   correct

Do not use a joining stroke. The letters **Va** could look like **Ua**.

incorrect   correct

Do not use a joining stroke. The letters **Pa** could look like **Ra**.

incorrect   correct

Make a looping stroke. The **K** could look like **X**.

incorrect   correct

Slant up to the right. Then loop and curve down to touch the bottom line and pass through the stem. The **S** could look like **D**.

ADDITIONAL PRACTICE

SENTENCES

A. Tell whether each word group is a *sentence* or *not a sentence*.

Example:
At the top of the map.

  not a sentence

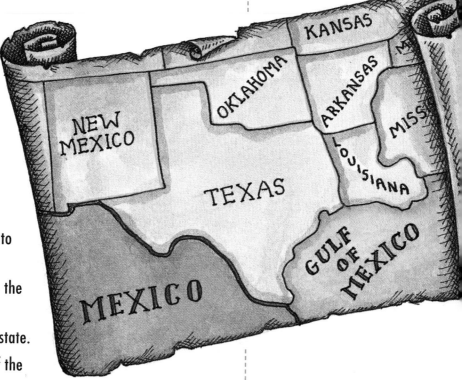

1. Gena looked at the map.

2. Find New Mexico.

3. She pointed to Arizona.

4. José went to the map.

5. The nearest state.

6. Lies north of the equator.

7. Everyone learned the names of mountain chains.

8. The longest river in the United States.

9. The states along the coast of the Gulf of Mexico.

10. Gena confused Kansas and Nebraska.

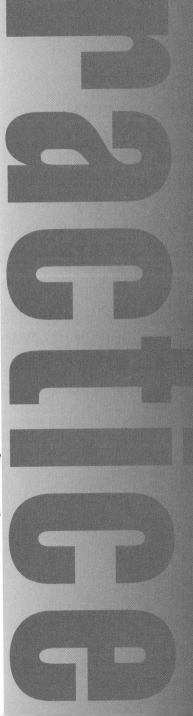

B. If a group of words is a sentence, write it correctly. Capitalize the first word, and end the sentence with a period. If the group is not a sentence, write *not a sentence.*

Example:
the capital of Illinois is Springfield

> *The capital of Illinois is Springfield.*

11. we memorized the capitals of all of the states
12. everyone knew the capital of Arkansas
13. the capital is not always the largest city in the state
14. you should picture the map in your mind
15. the left side is the west side
16. right through the middle of the country
17. that river empties into the Gulf of Mexico
18. the Hudson River valley
19. three people found Delaware right away
20. a map of the thirteen original colonies

DECLARATIVE, INTERROGATIVE, EXCLAMATORY, AND IMPERATIVE SENTENCES

A. Read each sentence. Tell whether it is *declarative, interrogative, exclamatory,* or *imperative.*

Example:
What is the size of the floor?

interrogative

1. How much paint will we need?
2. Everyone will help on Saturday.
3. Can your brother paint?
4. The barn is quite large.
5. What kind of red paint is that?
6. What a bright color that is!
7. Give that brush to me.
8. Will we finish by sundown?
9. Look at your watch.
10. What a lot of fun that was!

B. Write each sentence. Begin and end each sentence correctly.

11. what kind of vegetables will grow here
12. how many rows of tomato plants do you want
13. you will need string
14. spade the ground first
15. we should pull those weeds
16. weeds keep sunlight away from the vegetables
17. what are those dandelions doing here
18. water these little plants carefully
19. bring that large watering can over here
20. these plants need lots of moisture
21. look for my hoe
22. put the garden tools in the garage
23. what a lot of work a garden is
24. do you enjoy working with plants
25. homegrown vegetables taste so wonderful

Practice

SUBJECTS AND PREDICATES

A. Read each sentence. Tell whether the underlined part is the subject or the predicate of the sentence.

Example:
The automobiles ahead of us <u>were not moving</u>.

 predicate

1. <u>The highway</u> was covered with water.

2. Martina <u>slowed down quickly</u>.

3. <u>She</u> looked at the cars ahead of us.

4. <u>Two of the cars</u> had water up to the door windows.

5. Martina <u>signaled to the cars behind us</u>.

6. Every car <u>backed up</u>.

7. <u>All of the drivers</u> turned their cars around.

8. Martina <u>followed them to Highway 17</u>.

9. <u>The cars all</u> took the alternate route to high ground.

10. We <u>arrived two hours late but safe and sound</u>.

B. Write each sentence. Then draw a vertical line between the subject and the predicate.

Example:
The heavy rains lasted for three days and nights.

The heavy rains | *lasted for three days and nights.*

11. The marshy ground was soaked with water.
12. The garbage truck was due in about thirty minutes.
13. Elvis needed to walk to the garbage cans in the back.
14. He pulled on his long rubber boots and his poncho.
15. The garbage bags were heavy.
16. He looked funny sloshing through the soggy grass.
17. One of the garbage bags broke.
18. Aunt Susan laughed out loud at the sight.
19. Elvis almost fell twice.
20. The garbage was placed in the cans despite the driving rain and spongy soil.
21. The pickup truck didn't arrive on time.
22. The two men on the truck complained about the wet roads.
23. We were glad to be inside.
24. Father grumbled about the amount of rain.
25. The birds found plenty of worms for their supper that night.

COMPLETE SUBJECTS AND SIMPLE SUBJECTS

A. Write each sentence. Underline the complete subject. Then write the simple subject.

Example:
The unexpected news surprised Vanna.

The unexpected news surprised Vanna.
  news

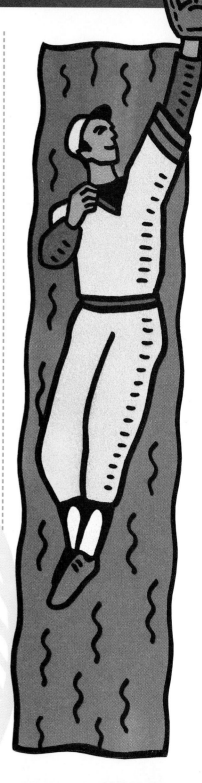

1. The right fielder on Vanna's team was sick.
2. The anxious coach asked her to substitute in right field.
3. The inexperienced player was pleased by the coach's request.
4. The other members of the team encouraged her.
5. The outfielder's mitt seemed almost too large.
6. The catcher on Vanna's team gave her some catching practice.
7. Outfielders on a baseball team often must catch fly balls on the run.
8. Vanna's speed as a runner was excellent.
9. Her only concern was about catching every ball.
10. Vanna took her place on the field.

B. Write each sentence. Draw a vertical line after the complete subject. Then underline the simple subject.

Example:
The young girl enjoyed playing on the baseball team.

   The young <u>girl</u> | *enjoyed playing on the baseball team.*

11. The very first batter struck out.

12. The pitcher on the mound concentrated on each pitch.

13. The first baseman caught a ground ball.

14. Vanna's team was ahead by two runs before the end of the third inning.

15. The ninth inning brought a crisis.

16. The other team almost tied the game.

17. The opposing team's pitcher got on base with a single to center field.

18. Their best hitter came to bat next.

19. She hit a high fly ball into right field.

20. Vanna's last-minute catch produced wild cheers from her teammates.

COMPLETE PREDICATES AND SIMPLE PREDICATES

A. Read each sentence. The complete predicate of each sentence is underlined. Write the simple predicate.

Example:
The young girl saw jewels of every color and size.

saw

1. Violetta looked in amazement at the beautiful light-blue stones.
2. The smiling clerk told Violetta about them.
3. The stones on the counter were called *turquoise*.
4. Violetta could not believe the careful workmanship.
5. No stone seemed the same as any other.
6. Each of the pieces was of a slightly different shape.
7. She saw other stones, such as lapis lazuli and amethyst.
8. The turquoise rings were her favorites.
9. The young girl made a decision right there and then.
10. She would learn the art of jewelry making.

174

B. Write each sentence. Draw a vertical line between the complete subject and the complete predicate. Then underline the simple predicate.

Example:

The Martins enjoyed the annual crafts fair.

The Martins | <u>enjoyed</u> the annual crafts fair.

11. The crafts exhibit contained many booths.
12. One of them was devoted to jewelry.
13. Rings, pendants, and bracelets glistened on a rack.
14. One of the most challenging tasks in jewelry making is the creation of the setting for the stone in a ring.
15. Some of the most unusual settings held pieces of amethyst or onyx.
16. The colors of the stones were quite varied.
17. A tiger-eye ring was especially beautiful.
18. All of the jewelry had been made by local craft workers.
19. Jewelry was a hobby for many of them.
20. Their work was comparable to that of a professional jeweler.

COMPOUND SUBJECTS AND COMPOUND PREDICATES

A. Read each sentence. Write the compound subject. Underline the word that joins the simple subjects.

Example:
The puppy and the kitten get along well with each other.

The puppy <u>and</u> the kitten

1. The veterinarian and her assistant examined the two animals.

2. Bud and Marissa smiled proudly.

3. A kitten or a puppy can be a special joy for a family.

4. Kittens and puppies usually are very curious.

5. Mr. Gundersen and his wife had bought their children a puppy.

6. A cat and one kitten found their way to the Gundersens' house.

7. Mrs. Gundersen or Marissa fed the animals on the back porch.

8. The kitten and its mother slept there every night.

9. Ads and phone calls produced no owner for the animals.

10. The cat, the puppy, and the kitten were soon the best of friends.

B. Read each sentence. Write the compound predicate, and underline the word that joins the simple predicates.

Example:
Tourists carry maps or ask questions.

  carry maps or ask questions

11. Miko squinted her eyes and studied the map.
12. She marked the map and walked toward the bus stop.
13. A woman stopped and asked Miko a question.
14. Miko understood the question but didn't know the answer.
15. The young girl and the woman laughed and shook hands.
16. Miko hurried to the bus stop and boarded the bus.
17. The girl stepped off the bus and crossed the street.
18. The museum was quite large and seemed very busy.
19. The line was long but moved quickly.
20. Miko bought a catalog and read about each painting.

SIMPLE AND COMPOUND SENTENCES

A. Identify each sentence as a *simple sentence* or a *compound sentence.*

Example:
Yoshi and John both play on the basketball team.

   simple sentence

1. Yoshi takes ballet lessons.
2. Ballet looks easy but is difficult.
3. John teased Yoshi, and Yoshi didn't like it.
4. Yoshi felt bad but didn't want to admit it.
5. Somehow he must find a solution to the problem.
6. He got a wonderful idea one day.
7. Yoshi asked John to his ballet class as a guest.
8. John refused, but Yoshi insisted.
9. Yoshi took John to class, and John had his first lesson.
10. The exercises were hard, and John couldn't do them.
11. Yoshi had great strength.
12. John's legs were weak.
13. The jumps took strength, and Yoshi jumped higher than anyone else.
14. John was surprised at Yoshi's ability and apologized to him for his unkind remarks.

B. Write each compound sentence. Draw a line under each simple sentence.

Example:
Art of any kind requires devotion, and artists must work hard.

Art of any kind requires devotion, and artists must work hard.

15. Dancing requires physical strength, and dancers sometimes have injuries.

16. Athletes often play with injuries, but dancers often have to perform with injuries, too.

17. Artists suffer in other ways, too, and pain is only one kind of hardship.

18. Dancers must pay for lessons, or they must win a scholarship.

19. Many dancers must work to earn money, but this work deprives them of practice time.

PRACTICE

NOUNS, COMMON NOUNS, AND PROPER NOUNS

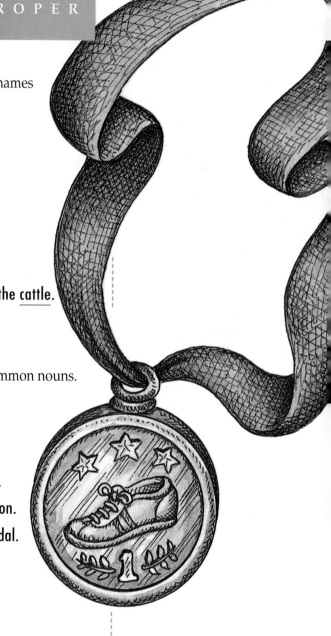

A. Tell whether each underlined word names a person, a place, a thing, or an idea.

Example:
The farmer looked at his field.

  farmer (person); field (place)

1. The chicken scratched for food.
2. The ground was very dry.
3. Water was scarce on our farm.
4. Our neighbor had to buy water for the cattle.
5. His family had great courage.

B. Read each sentence and write the common nouns.

Example:
The athlete was preparing for the race.

  athlete; race

6. Susan swam her last lap in the pool.
7. She was practicing for the competition.
8. Raven was also competing for a medal.
9. She is a runner, not a swimmer.
10. The girls work out each day.

C. Read each sentence and write the proper nouns.

Example:

My cousin Andrea just got back from hiking in the White Mountains.

 Andrea; White Mountains

11. These mountains are in northern New Hampshire.

12. Mount Washington, in the White Mountains, is the highest point in New England.

13. Andrea and her friends Mike and Miriam went up to Mount Chocorua.

14. They drove there from Lawrence, Massachusetts.

15. They went hiking along the Kancamagus Highway.

D. Write each proper noun and capitalize it correctly.

16. The lincoln memorial is very beautiful.

17. The white house is located on pennsylvania avenue.

18. While in washington, d.c., we saw a copy of the declaration of independence.

19. uncle ralph visited the house of representatives.

20. aunt margaret spoke with senator dianne feinstein.

SINGULAR AND PLURAL NOUNS

A. Read each sentence and write the singular nouns.

Example:
The woman dug up the dry, hard soil.

woman; soil

1. She planted the rosebush carefully.
2. Then she covered the roots with fresh dirt.
3. The garden was her favorite place.
4. From her porch, the woman could see a deer grazing.
5. Without enough rain, the plants would wither.

B. Read each sentence and write the plural nouns.

Example:
The recipe called for six potatoes.

potatoes

6. Two chefs chopped onions.
7. Fresh tomatoes and cucumbers lay on the table.
8. Slices of hot bread were put into baskets.
9. The stew cooked for more than two hours.
10. The vegetables turned to mush.

C. Proofread each sentence. Decide whether each underlined noun is used correctly or incorrectly. Rewrite each incorrect noun in the correct form.

Example:
Fall is a beautiful <u>seasons</u> of the year.

season

11. The <u>branch</u> of the trees begin to grow bare.

12. The <u>leaf</u> turn yellow and red.

13. The <u>days</u> are noticeably cooler.

14. Animals grow thick <u>coat</u> of hair.

15. <u>Squirrel</u> busily hunt for nuts.

16. You can find <u>jug</u> of fresh cider on the <u>shelves</u> of stores.

17. A frosty <u>morning</u> is a good time to have a <u>bowls</u> of hot oatmeal.

18. Many people travel to farms to pick <u>apple</u> and <u>pear</u>.

19. They put the fruit in <u>basket</u>.

20. A juicy apple is my favorite <u>snacks</u>.

21. Too little rain is not good for apple <u>trees</u>.

22. Too much <u>rainfalls</u> is bad for many <u>crop</u>.

23. Hot sunny days produce healthy <u>ear</u> of <u>corns</u>.

24. <u>Tornado</u> can destroy crops and farmland.

25. <u>Autumns</u> can be a <u>times</u> of rich or poor harvest.

POSSESSIVE NOUNS

A. Write the singular possessive form of each noun.

Example:
the parent

the parent's

1. the cow
2. the painter
3. the earth
4. the adult
5. Jupiter

6. Charles
7. the child
8. Trish
9. the orchestra
10. the worker

B. Write the plural possessive form of each noun.

Example:
the babies

the babies'

11. the women
12. the farmers
13. the dentists
14. the children
15. the gardeners

16. the sheep
17. the cubs
18. the troops
19. the principals
20. the porpoises

C. Tell whether the underlined possessive noun is singular or plural in form.

Example:

The sea cadets' lockers were cleaned.

plural possessive

21. The captain's order was obeyed.

22. The sailors' task was difficult.

23. The seamen's hands tugged at the anchor.

24. The winds blew more fiercely against the vessel's sails.

25. No one had seen the sun's rays for three days.

26. The ship's doctor himself was sick.

27. He worked on to save his companions' lives.

28. Across the water came the sounds of people's shouts.

29. The whalers' hearts were lifted.

30. In two months' time, the storm would be only a memory.

PRONOUNS AND ANTECEDENTS

A. Write the pronoun or pronouns in each sentence.

Example:
Roger looked at the flute he had just bought.

he

1. Roger said he was going to learn to play the flute.

2. Roger's sister Beth said she also wanted to play in the orchestra.

3. Roger's teacher said, "You must learn the fingering well."

4. She asked him to learn a new piece.

5. The music was difficult, and Roger practiced it for a long time.

6. Beth said she wanted to study the same piece of music.

7. Roger and Beth were nervous when they auditioned for the conductor.

8. She asked Roger to play the piece he had learned, and then she asked Beth to play it.

9. When they got home, Roger's parents had news for them.

10. They said, "Congratulations, Roger and Beth. You passed the audition."

B. Write the pronoun or pronouns in each sentence. Then write the antecedent of the pronoun.

Example:
In 1843 many people caught what they called "Oregon fever."

they—many people

11. The pioneers traveled along a route they called the Oregon Trail.

12. The trail was about 2,000 miles long, and it followed the Platte River.

13. The travelers followed the trail as they rode west.

14. The trail began in Missouri, and it crossed the Rocky Mountains.

15. One group had almost 1,000 people, and they rode in more than 120 wagons.

16. A special guide was hired, and he planned the details of the trip.

17. The pioneers took along 5,000 farm animals and used them for food.

18. Wagons traveled in a special order, and it never changed.

19. There might be night attacks, so drivers formed wagons into a circle to guard against them.

20. The pioneers crossed a river by fording it, driving the wagons and horses right into it at a shallow point.

SUBJECT PRONOUNS

A. Write the subject pronoun in each sentence.

Example:

We always learn something useful from Grandmother.

We

1. Yesterday I learned something new about cooking from Grandmother.

2. Before boiling potatoes, she cuts off a slice from the seed end.

3. You may wonder which is the seed end of a potato.

4. Well, it is the end not attached to the vine.

5. It becomes watery in the spring.

6. Potatoes may have watery ends, and then they get bruised.

7. I learned something else.

8. After potatoes are boiled, they should be left to steam in the pot for a while.

9. Grandmother says she uses potatoes to make shortcakes and puddings.

10. She saves on flour and uses less shortening.

B. Write the complete form of the underlined contraction in each sentence.

Example:
Guess where we're going!

we are

11. We're going to the historical museum on Saturday.
12. You'll enjoy the exhibit, too.
13. It's a display of old buggies and carriages.
14. They're examples of how people traveled in the 1800s.
15. I'll get you a ticket.
16. We're leaving early in the morning.
17. You'll even see a Conestoga wagon.
18. I'll bet riding in one was bumpy.
19. I'm sure the roads were unpaved.
20. You'd surely get wet in an open carriage in the rain.

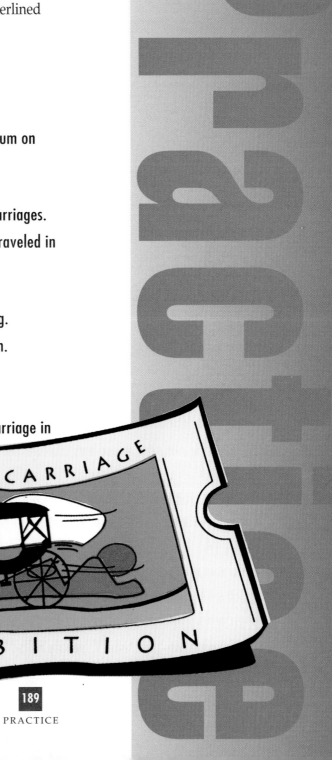

BUGGY AND CARRIAGE EXHIBITION

OBJECT PRONOUNS

C. Write the object pronoun in each sentence.

Example:
Some early laws that applied to horseless carriages might surprise you.

you

21. For example, the Red Flag Law in England in 1865 will amuse you.

22. Drivers of cars had to have a person walking ahead of them waving a red flag.

23. At night the person walking had to carry a red lantern with him.

24. The red objects helped folks on foot by warning them of the car.

25. The driver of a car could drive it no faster than four miles per hour.

26. Believe it or not, that speed was the legal limit until 1896!

27. Speeds gradually rose, so that by 1886 inventors had pushed them up to ten miles per hour.

28. Henry Ford's first automobile plant had only fifty people working in it.

29. The Model T and the Model A were two very popular cars, and Ford's company produced them.

30. The favorite was the Model T; people called it the "Tin Lizzie."

D. Write the reflexive pronoun in each sentence.

Example:
Before television, people amused themselves by listening to radio.

   themselves

31. At night a family would gather itself around a large radio.

32. Family members sat themselves down in chairs to listen.

33. Every household prided itself on its radio.

34. Stars of vaudeville changed themselves into radio comedians.

35. The first soap operas supported themselves by advertising laundry soap.

36. A radio audience had to imagine for itself the setting and action of the drama.

37. The sound effects booth was in itself a world of wonders.

38. Empty coconut shells could turn themselves into the sounds of horses' hooves.

39. To give the effect of fire, you got yourself some cellophane and crinkled it up.

40. I made myself a list of programs popular in the 1930s and the 1940s.

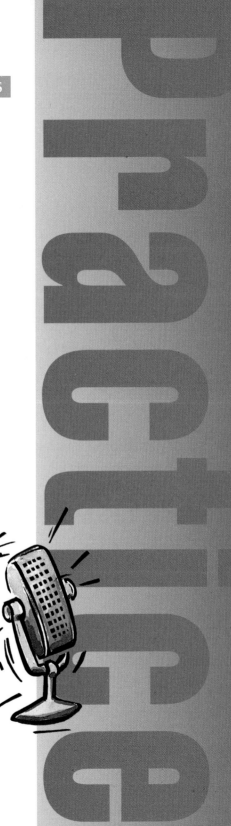

ADDITIONAL PRACTICE

POSSESSIVE PRONOUNS

A. Write the possessive pronoun in each sentence.

Example:

My aunt and uncle have lots of antiques.

My

1. They store the objects in their house and garage.
2. Aunt Ella owns an antique store near our house.
3. She has had her business for more than ten years.
4. She and Uncle Bert drive their large van to auctions.
5. His favorite antiques are unusual household objects from the nineteenth century.
6. Her collection includes old iceboxes and odd kitchen gadgets.
7. One of my favorites is a device for taking the pits out of cherries.
8. Father said his favorite was a machine for juicing carrots.
9. You might think that people drank the carrot juice for their health.
10. The carrot juice was used to color their homemade butter.

B. Write the possessive pronoun or pronouns in each sentence. Then tell whether the pronoun comes *before a noun* or *stands alone*.

Example:
My monthly bill is larger than hers.

   My—before a noun; hers—stands alone

11. The credit card originated because people drove their cars everywhere.

12. Every gasoline company wanted its customers to buy its brand of gas.

13. Customers could use their credit cards at gas stations nationwide.

14. The first general cards were issued for eating your dinner at a restaurant.

15. Today Dad has his credit cards.

16. Mother has hers, too.

17. Students in college often have theirs.

18. Your credit card has your picture on it.

19. Mine doesn't.

20. Yours has a special design, but hers is plain.

ADJECTIVES

A. Identify the adjectives and articles in each sentence.

Example:
Two stoves sat in the kitchen.

Two; the

1. Grandmother did the weekly washing on the coal-burning stove.

2. Washing was hard work for everyone.

3. Water was heated in big tubs on the stove.

4. Then the dirty clothes were put into the hot water.

5. Grandmother stirred the clothes with a wooden stick.

6. The soapy clothes were then moved to a second tub for rinsing.

7. The rinsed clothes were put through an old-fashioned wringer.

8. Two cylindrical wringers were pressed together as they turned.

9. The wooden wringers were turned by a crank.

10. Finally, the clean clothes were taken out and hung on a clothesline.

B. Identify the proper adjectives in each sentence. Then write the proper noun from which each is formed.

Example:
The earliest American immigrants were English people.

American (America); English (England)

11. Other European settlers came soon after.

12. From the seventeenth century to the nineteenth century, few immigrants came to American shores.

13. Asian immigrants helped build America in the 1900s.

14. Chinese immigrants labored to build the railroads.

15. Swedish settlers farmed the plains.

16. Many people have Scandinavian ancestors.

17. German immigrants began farms in Wisconsin and Minnesota.

18. Italian people came to America in the late nineteenth century.

19. Along with Irish immigrants, they settled in the large cities of the East.

20. Spanish people were early settlers of what is now California.

COMPARING WITH ADJECTIVES

A. Complete each sentence by writing the correct form of the adjective in parentheses ( ).

Example:
The first skyscraper in New York was also the (high) building in the world.

   highest

1. The (old) building materials were wood and stone.

2. The use of iron and steel made it possible to build (tall) buildings than ever before.

3. The (mighty) advance in the building of skyscrapers was the elevator.

4. Climbing stairs is a (hard) way to get to the top of a building than riding in an elevator.

5. The (early) skyscraper was a twelve-story building in Chicago.

6. By 1889 the world's (high) structure was the Eiffel Tower in Paris.

7. The ground in Chicago is not the (firm) type of soil for tall buildings.

8. The soil there is (loose) and (wet) than it is in New York.

9. In New York, much of the island of Manhattan is composed of rock, the (strong) foundation possible.

10. The Empire State Building, at a height of 1,250 feet, was the (high) skyscraper of its time.

B. Write *more* or *most* to complete the comparison in each sentence.

Example:
Before the railroad, the _____ useful form of transportation was by waterway.

   most

11. In Great Britain, the _____ important use for canals was carrying coal.

12. Perhaps the _____ unusual canal of all flowed directly into the coal mines.

13. Carrying coal was _____ expensive before canals were built.

14. Canals soon crisscrossed England, making many businesses _____ profitable than ever.

15. It was _____ difficult for horses to pull loads over muddy roads than along canals.

(continued on next page)

COMPARING WITH ADJECTIVES

16. On land the _____ sizable load a horse could pull was about 250 pounds.

17. On a canal, the same horse could pull loads up to 240 times _____ massive than that.

18. The _____ ambitious canals required the building of many locks.

19. Using the locks, boats went from low places to locations that were _____ elevated, and vice versa.

20. The _____ challenging task was to raise or lower the water level.

21. The technique used was _____ complicated than you might think.

22. The _____ mysterious part of canal building is how locks were developed.

23. The _____ ancient drawings of locks were made by Leonardo da Vinci.

24. One of the _____ puzzling questions involves how locks opened.

25. To the Italians, opening lock gates vertically seemed _____ efficient than doing so horizontally.

C. Complete each sentence by writing the correct form of the adjective shown in parentheses ( ).

Example:
To go short distances, railroads are (good) than airplanes or automobiles.

better

26. The speed of trains is (good) than ever before.

27. The (good) thing of all about trains is that you can travel from the center of one city to the center of another.

28. My grandfather said taking the Interurban from Urbana, Illinois, to Decatur, Illinois, was (good) than driving.

29. He said that the (good) reason to have those trains was that they connected all the midsize cities in Illinois.

30. In some ways, rail travel is (good) than it used to be.

31. In other ways, it is (bad).

32. Grandfather thinks rail travel will be (good) than ever because of new high-speed trains.

33. Travel conditions on early railroads were far (bad) than they are today.

34. The (bad) thing of all about early trains was the thick smoke that poured out of the engines.

35. I can't imagine anything (good) than zipping from Los Angeles to San Francisco in less than three hours.

VERBS

A. Identify the verb in each sentence.

Example:
Our house has a large fireplace.

has

1. Another name for a fireplace is a hearth.

2. Hearths provided heat for the living room.

3. No one strayed far from the fireplace in winter.

4. Fireplaces often had two or three hooks.

5. Each hook swung away from the fire.

B. Identify the action verb in each sentence.

Example:
I found these books in the attic.

found

6. This diary contains a lot of our family history.

7. It tells a fascinating story.

8. Our ancestors traveled a long way.

9. They settled in the Middle West.

10. That trunk holds tintypes and photographs from the old days.

11. Old photographs fade.

12. Grandfather took many pictures of his bride-to-be.

13. This picture shows my grandmother in a bathing suit.

14. These bathing suits covered one's entire body.

15. Women wore bathing hats as well.

C. Identify the linking verb in each sentence.

Example:
That woman looks familiar.

looks

16. Yes, she is my grandmother.

17. She is also the woman in this photograph.

18. The occasion was a Fourth of July picnic.

19. Family reunions became a tradition.

20. Our family remains close.

21. That tree in the background was only an acorn in 1888.

22. It became a huge oak tree.

23. This photo of the tree is my favorite.

24. The tree seems young and sturdy.

25. It is healthy even today.

MAIN VERBS AND HELPING VERBS

A. Identify the main verb in each sentence.

Example:

In July you can see lots of fireflies.

see

1. July has always reminded me of fireflies.
2. You can see them every evening then.
3. I have always connected them with the Fourth of July.
4. We would watch the fireworks then.
5. Between the displays, the fireflies would dance.
6. Fireflies are also called *lightning bugs*.
7. A firefly can be considered a beetle.
8. Fireflies have always seemed like little UFOs to me.
9. You will spy them in one place.
10. Then suddenly they will have moved to another place.

B. Identify the helping verb and the main verb in each sentence.

Example:
The circus will always be my favorite entertainment.

will; be

11. Do you see that little car?
12. A clown is driving it.
13. The car is coming toward us.
14. It has stopped right in front of us.
15. The door has opened.
16. The clown is stepping out of the car.
17. What did you say?
18. I have counted four clowns so far.
19. Eight clowns have emerged from that little car.
20. How do they squeeze into that small space?
21. No one would believe it.
22. Do you see a hole in the ground anywhere?
23. Can more clowns be in there?
24. I have now counted twelve clowns.
25. Twelve clowns can fit in a car so small!

TENSE

A. Tell whether the verb in each sentence is in the *present tense*, in the *past tense*, or in the *future tense*.

Example:

I stand in front of the audience.

   stand – present tense

1. The play will be next week.
2. I have the leading role.
3. We rehearsed for four weeks.
4. I memorized all my lines.
5. My best friend helped me.
6. I will tell you the story of the play.
7. No one believes me.
8. I come from another planet.
9. I wear green makeup.
10. You will be surprised!

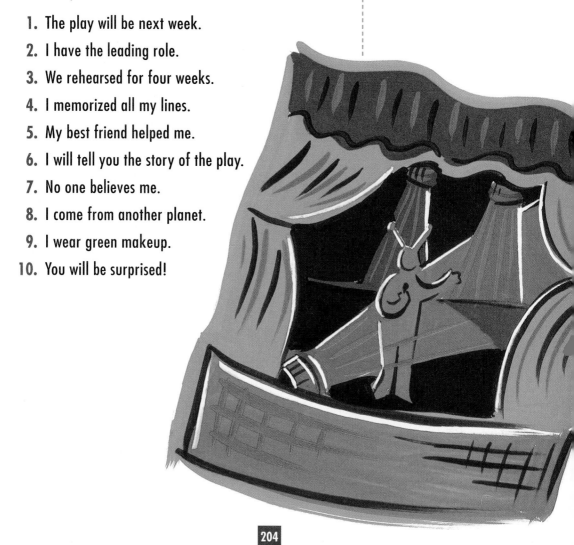

B. Complete each sentence correctly by writing the present-tense form of the verb shown in parentheses ( ).

Example:
Art (be) my hobby.

   is

11. I (begin) art classes today.
12. My teacher (be) Mr. Nunez.
13. I (have) all my equipment.
14. The class (meet) in a large studio.
15. My sister Lise (paint) well.
16. She (observe) objects very carefully.
17. Now I (notice) things differently, too.
18. I (be) aware of details.
19. This shade of blue (look) right.
20. Strong colors often (go) well together.
21. Mr. Nunez (teach) three classes.
22. Lise and I (be) in two of them.
23. Lise (sketch) like a professional.
24. Her sense of humor (show) here.
25. (Be) this a drawing of you?

P A S T   T E N S E

 A. Complete each sentence correctly by writing the past-tense form of the verb shown in parentheses ( ).

Example:
We (park) our car in the lot.

parked

1. Many people (wait) in line.
2. The water (look) cool.
3. Lifeguards (watch) the swimmers.
4. The toddlers (play) in shallow water.
5. Their mothers (watch) them carefully.
6. I (enjoy) my swimming lessons last year.
7. The slide (end) in the water.
8. I (climb) up the ladder.
9. The water (moisten) the surface of the slide.
10. The water (cool) me.

11. The person before me (splash) in the water.

12. She (paddle) in the waves.

13. I (reach) for the edges of the slide.

14. I (push) myself off down the slide.

15. Before long, I (plop) into the pool.

16. My mother and sister (laugh) at me.

17. Our dog Rusty (bark) at me noisily.

18. Then my sister and I (join) a water polo game.

19. She (place) me on her shoulders.

20. Soon I (tumble) off into the water.

21. By noontime, we all (want) food.

22. We (unpack) our picnic basket under the trees.

23. Rusty (wag) his tail eagerly.

24. The food (taste) good.

25. Our day at the pool (end) before sundown.

IRREGULAR VERBS

A. Complete each sentence correctly by writing the present-tense form of the verb shown in parentheses ( ).

Example:
Our school (have) a music club.

has

1. Robin (bring) her guitar to our weekly meetings.

2. She (be) our accompanist.

3. We (sing) songs at each meeting.

4. Robin (do) very well on the guitar.

5. Hers (be) an acoustic guitar.

6. Our teacher, Mrs. Melendez, (make) us rehearse frequently.

7. She (know) music very well.

8. At each meeting she (give) us harmony lessons.

9. Tonight we (begin) practicing for a concert.

10. Robin (write) original music for us.

11. Music (make) me happy.

12. (Be) you a singer?

13. Most of our songs (be) in three parts.

14. Three-part music (be) difficult.

15. Frank usually (take) the alto part.

16. Sally (have) a higher voice.

17. Sally and four others (sing) first soprano.

18. Our chorus (do) very well with so few singers.

19. We are excited when we (give) our first concert of the year.

20. Frank (do) our posters.

21. This one from last year (be) my favorite.

22. It (have) four colors.

23. The musical notes (begin) an old song.

24. My mother (know) all the words.

25. The first part of the song (go) like this.

26. Val always (eat) something before singing.

27. Everyone usually (drink) something during rehearsals.

28. Who (have) an extra ticket for the concert?

29. Sally (do).

30. There (be) no more empty seats.

ADDITIONAL PRACTICE

IRREGULAR VERBS

B. Complete each sentence correctly by writing the past-tense form of the irregular verb shown in parentheses ( ).

Example:
Our family (go) to an amusement park last week.

  went

31. The fun house (be) our first stop.
32. I (see) myself in the funny mirrors.
33. Then we (ride) in a little train through a long tunnel.
34. I (be) scared of the horrible sights.
35. Dad (bring) a camera.
36. He (take) pictures of some of the eerie creatures.
37. The train (make) a sharp turn.
38. It almost (run) off the tracks.
39. I (think) I would faint.
40. The experience (give) me goose bumps.
41. After that, we (have) lunch.
42. At first, I (eat) nothing.
43. I (be) hungry, though.
44. We (bring) a picnic lunch.
45. By two o'clock, the sky (grow) cloudy.
46. Next (come) the rides.
47. My brother (see) the roller coaster.

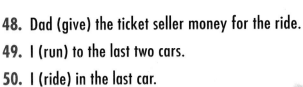

48. Dad (give) the ticket seller money for the ride.

49. I (run) to the last two cars.

50. I (ride) in the last car.

51. From the top, we (see) the whole park.

52. The first drop (be) the steepest one.

53. The passengers (make) a lot of noise.

54. The whole trip (take) almost five minutes.

55. We (go) on the roller coaster two more times.

56. After that, we (come) to the Ferris wheel.

57. Dad (take) us all on that ride, too.

58. The wheel (do) a funny thing.

59. When we were at the top, it (come) to a stop.

60. That real incident (be) scarier than the silly things in the fun house.

ADDITIONAL PRACTICE

FUTURE TENSE

A. Write the future-tense form of the verb shown in parentheses ( ) to complete each sentence.

Example:
School (begin) in two weeks.

  will begin

1. I (be) in the fifth grade then.
2. My sister Andrea and I (attend) a new school.
3. A bus (take) us there.
4. Many of my friends (go) with us.
5. Andrea (be) in the sixth grade.
6. This (make) Andrea's second year at that school.
7. We both (have) new teachers.
8. Her former teacher (be) my new one.
9. In October, auditions (begin) for Student Night.
10. I (try) for a part in the show.

11. Andrea (sing) two numbers.

12. Our parents (come) to the opening performance.

13. Other relatives (arrive) just in time for the final performance.

14. My cousin and I (open) the show.

15. We (do) a tap dance.

16. We (wear) tap shoes and flashy suits.

17. In all, forty students (perform).

18. The show (raise) money for the art and music departments.

19. Some of that money (go) for new instruments.

20. This year Andrea (study) the clarinet.

CLICKITY CLICK   CLICKITY CLICK

ADVERBS

A. For each sentence, identify the adverb that describes each underlined word. Then write whether the adverb tells *how, when, where,* or *to what extent.*

Example:
Our dog Sasha is a very <u>loving</u> pet.

  very; to what extent

1. Sasha <u>lay</u> quietly on the rug.
2. She <u>slept</u> there in the afternoon.
3. She suddenly <u>lifted</u> her head.
4. She <u>rose</u> quickly from her spot.
5. She <u>went</u> to the door anxiously.
6. I soon <u>heard</u> a knock at the door.
7. Josepha, our mail carrier, pleasantly <u>surprised</u> us with a package.
8. Sasha <u>greeted</u> her noisily.
9. The happy dog <u>stood</u> there wagging her tail.
10. Josepha <u>scratched</u> Sasha lovingly under the chin.
11. Sasha always <u>hears</u> every sound.
12. Sounds often <u>wake</u> her from sleep.
13. She regularly <u>announces</u> visitors.
14. She is very <u>happy</u> to see our friends.
15. She is extremely <u>cautious</u> with strangers.

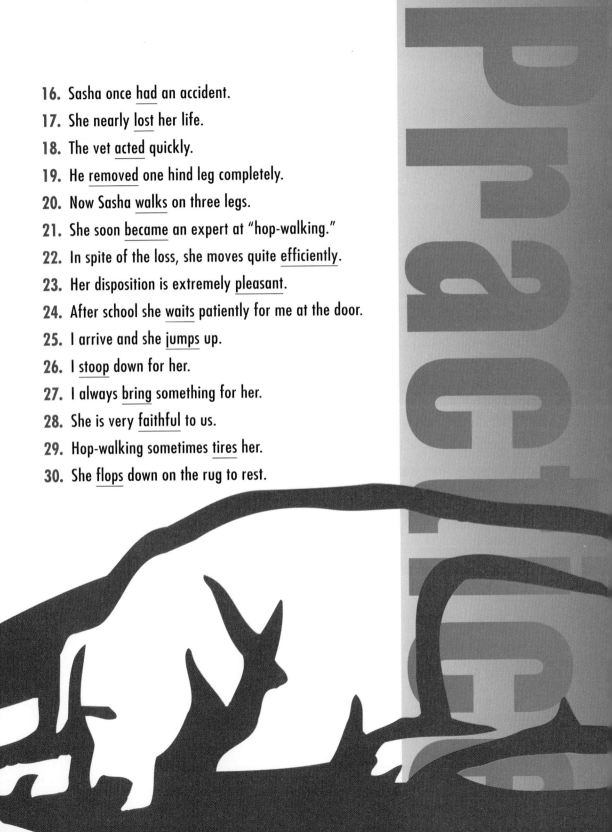

16. Sasha once <u>had</u> an accident.

17. She nearly <u>lost</u> her life.

18. The vet <u>acted</u> quickly.

19. He <u>removed</u> one hind leg completely.

20. Now Sasha <u>walks</u> on three legs.

21. She soon <u>became</u> an expert at "hop-walking."

22. In spite of the loss, she moves quite <u>efficiently</u>.

23. Her disposition is extremely <u>pleasant</u>.

24. After school she <u>waits</u> patiently for me at the door.

25. I arrive and she <u>jumps</u> up.

26. I <u>stoop</u> down for her.

27. I always <u>bring</u> something for her.

28. She is very <u>faithful</u> to us.

29. Hop-walking sometimes <u>tires</u> her.

30. She <u>flops</u> down on the rug to rest.

COMPARING WITH ADVERBS

A. Write the form of the adverb shown in parentheses ( ) that correctly completes each sentence.

Example:
This plant blooms (late) than that one.

later

1. Plants grow (fast) with fertilizer than they do without fertilizer.
2. Dig this hole (deep) into the ground than the last one.
3. Make it (wide) than you did before.
4. In this country, spring comes (early) of all in the South.
5. Plants suffer from frost (hard) of all in the northernmost states.
6. Can you stand (close) than that to this sapling?
7. You must grasp the trunk (high) than this, or the tree will fall.
8. We planted saplings (late) than usual this year.
9. This year's crop will mature (soon) than last year's.
10. The wet weather lasted (long) than usual.

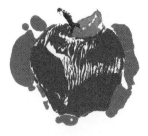

B. Write the form of the adverb shown in parentheses ( ) that correctly completes each sentence.

Example:
Forecasters can predict weather (accurately) than before.

   more accurately

11. A car can skid (quickly) on icy streets than on rainy streets.

12. Radio newscasts provide weather updates (regularly) than do TV reports.

13. Weather forecasts can change (surprisingly) of all when wind patterns change.

14. Some parts of the nation get large amounts of rain (often) than others.

15. Forecasters can predict (accurately) of all in places where conditions change slowly.

C. Complete each sentence with the form of *well* or *badly* that makes sense.

Example:
Do large solar panels work (well) than small ones?

   better

16. Solar panels work (well) of all with lots of sunshine.

17. They operate (bad) of all in cloudy conditions.

18. I think I like solar panels (well) than windmills.

19. Geothermal energy may do (well) than either wind or solar power.

ADDITIONAL PRACTICE

A. Write the word shown in parentheses ( ) that correctly completes each sentence. Avoid double negatives.

Example:

Not many people (have, haven't) seen a forest fire.

have

1. A forest fire isn't (never, ever) the end of a forest.

2. The little trees and bushes can't (ever, never) get much sunshine in an old forest.

3. The biggest trees don't (never, ever) let the sunshine in.

4. If the big trees don't die or burn, the little saplings can't (ever, never) grow.

5. No fire (never, ever) starts without a cause.

6. There doesn't have to be (no, any) human cause for a fire.

7. Haven't you (never, ever) heard of lightning causing a fire?

8. Not (everyone, no one) remembers that.

9. Didn't (nobody, anybody) show you pictures of Mount St. Helens after the eruption?

10. I haven't (never, ever) seen so many trees burned.

11. The damage wasn't caused by (no, any) forest fire.

12. I didn't have (any, no) idea that lava could be so destructive.

13. You couldn't imagine (anything, nothing) more surprising than that volcano now.

14. There's not (no, any) ground that's still barren.

15. Why didn't (no one, anyone) show us those pictures until now?

16. Aren't there (no, any) pictures of Yellowstone National Park?

17. Didn't (nobody, anybody) tell you about the fire there?

18. After the fire, animals couldn't find (any, no) grass to eat.

19. There (was, wasn't) no vegetation where the fire had burned.

20. Fortunately, it didn't take (any, no) time until new grass began to sprout.

PREPOSITIONS AND PREPOSITIONAL PHRASES

A. Identify the preposition in each sentence.

Example:

Do you know about the Endangered Species Act?

   about

1. Some species couldn't survive without it.

2. Have you ever seen a falcon in flight?

3. The falcon almost became extinct from DDT poisoning.

4. The peregrine falcon is loved for its graceful flight.

5. It can dive at great speeds.

B. The underlined word or words in each sentence are the object of a preposition. Write the preposition for each object.

Example:

Fifteen inches is the length of an average <u>falcon</u>.

   of

6. Have you ever seen a falcon dive toward the <u>earth</u>?

7. A peregrine falcon has a wingspan of forty <u>inches</u>.

8. In the <u>1970s</u> there were fewer than 2,000 falcons.

9. The effect of <u>DDT</u> prevented falcon reproduction.

10. The falcon population has increased by eight <u>thousand</u>.

11. The increase in <u>numbers</u> is quite impressive.
12. The U.S. Fish and Wildlife Service may remove the species from its endangered <u>list</u>.
13. Falcons can even be seen on <u>Golden Gate Bridge</u>.
14. I have seen them also in <u>Boston</u>.
15. They have adapted well to these unusual <u>homes</u>.

C. Identify the prepositional phrase in each sentence. Name the preposition.

Example:
Trainers of falcons are called *falconers.*
   of falcons; of

16. Training them takes a good deal of time.
17. The birds must often wear hoods over their heads.
18. The falcon flies away into the sky.
19. Then it must return to its trainer.
20. Falcons are prized for their hunting ability.
21. Some people do not like birds of prey.
22. They do not realize the importance of natural predators.
23. Keeping animal populations in balance is important.
24. Preying birds, or raptors, help in this process.
25. Every creature has an important place in nature.

TROUBLESOME WORDS

A. Choose the word in parentheses ( ) that correctly completes each sentence.

Example:
I have not been performing (good, well) lately.

well

1. This chicken soup tastes (good, well).

2. Many more than just (too, to, two) folk remedies for colds are known.

3. I suppose (there, they're, their) is some good in them all.

4. Some say chicken soup will make you (good, well).

5. Experts say (its, it's) the selenium in the soup.

6. This element is a (good, well) substance to take for a cold.

7. (Their, There, They're) is another helpful thing to do when you are sick.

8. Doctors say that drinking fluids is a (well, good) thing for a cold.

9. (Your, You're) never wrong to do that.

10. Drinking fluids is (well, good) for you most of the time.

11. (To, Too, Two) me, fluids are enough to cure a cold.

12. But (there, their, they're) are still more remedies.

13. Grandmother would always plaster (your, you're) chest with a mustard plaster.

14. It was supposed to make you (good, well) overnight.

15. It certainly smelled awful (to, two, too) me.

16. Did your grandmother do that, (to, too, two)?

17. (You're, Your) not joking, are you?

18. (Its, It's) no coincidence, I guess.

19. A lot of people used home remedies to help themselves get (good, well).

20. Rest is also an important part of (your, you're) recovery.

21. (Its, It's) no fun lying in bed.

22. But sleep can help make you (good, well).

23. Isn't laughter also (good, well) for you?

24. Yes, laughter is (you're, your) best friend.

25. Laughing is something I do (well, good).

TROUBLESOME WORDS

B. Choose the word or words in parentheses ( ) that correctly complete each sentence.

Example:
A proper diet should play (its, it's) part in (good, well) health.

> *its; good*

26. Food that is (well, good) for you should taste (good, well), too.

27. That's not (to, too, two) much (to, too, two) ask, is it?

28. (Its, It's) not easy (to, too, two) eat food that tastes terrible.

29. If food doesn't taste (good, well), it doesn't matter whether (there, their, they're) is great nutrition in it.

30. I'm glad (your, you're) in agreement with that.

31. Do you see that restaurant down (their, they're, there)?

32. (Its, It's) a popular restaurant with (good, well) chefs.

33. I think (their, they're, there) secret is (well, good) seasoning.

34. (They're, Their, There) always busy down (their, they're, there) in the restaurant.

35. I think (your, you're) wallet could take it.

36. Would you like to eat (their, there, they're) sometime?

37. "(Good, Well) food (good, well) prepared" is (their, they're, there) motto.

38. (Its, It's) a goal of mine (to, too, two) run a restaurant.

39. The (to, too, two) of us would make a great team.

40. My uncle says (your, you're) never (to, two, too) young to plan such a thing.

41. He says (they're, their, there) is always room for a good restaurant.

42. I myself think (their, there, they're) are (to, two, too) many bad restaurants around.

43. You shouldn't serve people (two, to, too) much food.

44. Less is more, when it comes (to, too, two) (well, good) cooking.

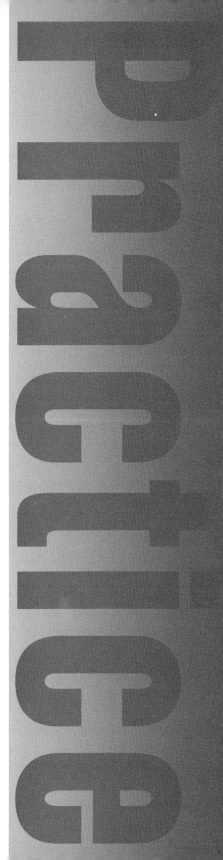

PUNCTUATION: COMMA

A. Write each sentence, adding commas where they are needed.

Example:
The three planets farthest from the sun are Uranus Neptune and Pluto.

The three planets farthest from the sun are Uranus, Neptune, and Pluto.

1. Yes each of the planets rotates on an axis.

2. Lucy name the planet nearest the sun.

3. Yes there are nine planets in all.

4. Oh I believe the two largest planets are Jupiter and Saturn.

5. Well the four planets nearest the sun are called terrestrial planets.

6. They are Mercury Venus Earth and Mars.

7. Yes the atmospheres of these planets contain mostly nitrogen and carbon dioxide.

8. No John the other planets have atmospheres made up mostly of four other gases.

9. Those four gases are helium hydrogen methane and ammonia.

10. Yes Marcia Earth is the only planet with a large amount of oxygen.

11. Yes astronomers believe there are planets around other stars in the universe.

12. Did you know Cecilie that there are more than 100 billion stars in our galaxy?

13. Yes the name of our galaxy is the Milky Way.

14. More than 100 billion galaxies can be seen Ned.

15. Yes that is an amazingly large number.

16. Which way do the planets move Penny as we look at them?

17. Yes Penny they move from east to west.

18. The three planets you can see most easily are Venus Jupiter and Saturn.

19. Mercury's year is only 88 days long Ted.

20. Well that's just about one-fourth as long as a year on the planet Earth.

21. Yes the astronomer Ptolemy thought the Earth was the center of the universe.

22. Juan his theory was accepted for more than 1,000 years.

23. Well it was not until 1543 that this view changed.

24. Copernicus was a student of mathematics law and medicine.

25. Ptolemy Copernicus and Kepler were important in early astronomy.

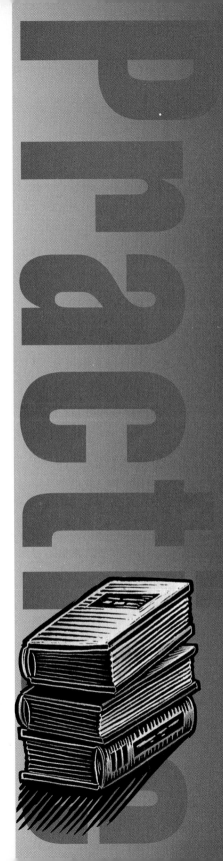

PUNCTUATION: COMMA

B. Add a comma to each compound sentence where it is needed. Not all are compound sentences.

Example:

This telescope is strong but that star is quite far away.

This telescope is strong, but that star is quite far away.

26. The astronomy club meets once a month and students go on field trips three times a year.

27. Once we went to an observatory but the telescope could not produce good pictures.

28. Telescopes are aimed at stars but scientists cannot always "see" the objects in space.

29. There are good observatories in the United States but the light here is too bright.

30. Light from cities can cause problems for scientists and other observers.

31. People in cities need to see at night but street lamps affect telescopes.

32. Some cities use yellow street lights and these lights do not cause problems for telescopes.

33. White street lights interfere with the view and scientists cannot use their telescopes.

34. Dark nights are best for observing stars and other objects in the sky.

35. Astronomers have to wait for good conditions or they must go to distant places.

36. Some scientists travel to Peru to observe the skies.

37. There is light in these places but it is much less bright.

38. Telescopes in the United States are expensive and they stand idle.

39. Some of the best telescopes in the world are here but they cannot be used.

40. Scientists used to drive just a few miles to see the stars but now they must fly hundreds of miles.

41. The nearest stars are visible without telescopes or binoculars.

42. Light from distant stars has traveled far and some stars are millions of light-years away.

43. Light travels about 186,000 miles per second and that is quite an amazing speed.

44. You can multiply to see how many miles it travels in a year but you would need a lot of paper to do your figuring.

45. I tried the problem on my calculator and the figures ran off the screen.

DIALOGUE

A. Write each sentence. Add quotation marks where they are needed.

Example:

When are you leaving? asked Ron.

"When are you leaving?" asked Ron.

1. We have to be at the airport by 3:00 P.M., replied Flora.

2. It takes time to check in, her mother said.

3. Yes, said Ron's father, you have to go through a metal detector.

4. Before that, said Flora, we have to check our bags.

5. I wish I were going with you, said Ron.

6. You just got back from a trip yourself, said Flora's mother.

7. I know, said Ron. We went to Chicago.

8. The plane was not in the air long, said Ron.

9. Ron's father said, Yes, it took longer to get to the airport than it did to fly to Chicago!

10. In Chicago, Ron added, there is a rapid-transit train that goes downtown from the airport.

11. Flora asked, Did you take the train?

12. Ron's father said, No, we were not going downtown.

13. Our destination was Evanston, Ron explained. My aunt lives there.

14. Did you see any sights while you were there? asked Flora's mother.

15. Oh, we certainly did, said Ron's father.

16. The first day we went to the Brookfield Zoo, said Ron.

17. That zoo is quite large, said Flora's mother.

18. It covers quite a bit of ground, said Ron, like the zoos in San Diego and in the Bronx, New York.

19. The next day we went to the Museum of Science and Industry, said Ron's father.

20. Ron added, That place is so large that you can't see it all in one day.

21. I don't think you're supposed to, laughed Flora's mother.

22. People go back to see different exhibits, I guess, said Ron.

23. Well, said Flora's mother, we must get out to the airport.

24. Bring me back a souvenir from Disney World, Flora, said Ron.

25. Don't you worry, Ron, replied Flora. I will.

TITLES

A. Write the titles in the following sentences correctly.

Example:
Where is the new copy of the national geographic magazine?

National Geographic

1. It's over there on the table next to newsweek.
2. I want to read the article entitled space shuttles.
3. I think time magazine also has an article about space stations.
4. It's called shuttling around earth.
5. I still remember the movie close encounters of the third kind.
6. I read a poem about space called worlds out there.
7. It's in a book entitled inner and outer space.
8. Did you watch that TV program on nova?
9. Let's watch star trek v tonight.
10. Oh, I forgot and rented indiana jones and the temple of doom.
11. Don is going to watch a rerun of star wars.
12. José wants to finish the puzzle in the New York times.

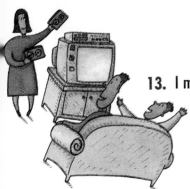

13. I may bring aunt liz a videocassette of flash gordon.

14. She might like around the world in 80 days.

15. I'll bet dad would like this one called touring america's national parks.

16. Yes, I read an article about it in AAA world.

17. Let's not forget to watch jeopardy tonight.

18. Later we can watch beauty and the beast.

19. Don't you have to finish reading that story, the gift of the magi?

20. I already finished reading that and a poem called chicago by carl sandburg.

ADDITIONAL PRACTICE

ABBREVIATIONS

A. Write the abbreviation of each term. Use a dictionary if you need to.

Example:
Boulevard

Blvd.

1. Alabama
2. Michigan
3. Virginia
4. New Mexico
5. California
6. Texas
7. Massachusetts
8. Connecticut
9. Maine
10. Monday

11. Saturday
12. Tuesday
13. Wednesday
14. 5 inches
15. 12 feet
16. 1,200 meters
17. 2 quarts
18. 4 gallons
19. 5 pounds
20. 14 ounces

21. President Clinton

22. Governor Richards

23. Reverend Jesse Jackson

24. Doctor Amy Chang

25. Mister James Mendez

26. General Omar Bradley

27. Captain MacIntosh

28. October 13

29. January 22

30. August 20

31. September 13

32. Bond Street

33. River Road

34. Michigan Avenue

35. Sunset Drive

36. Columbia University

37. Washington High School

38. United States

39. Mount McKinley

40. Saint Augustine

Note: Italic page numbers in main headings refer to additional practice.